Ferdinand Magellan

and the Quest to Circle the Globe

Explorers of New Lands

Christopher Columbus
and the Discovery of the Americas

Hernándo Cortés
and the Fall of the Aztecs

Francis Drake
and the Oceans of the World

Francisco Coronado
and the Seven Cities of Gold

Ferdinand Magellan
and the Quest to Circle the Globe

Hernando de Soto
and His Expeditions Across the Americas

Francisco Pizarro
and the Conquest of the Inca

Marco Polo
and the Realm of Kublai Khan

Juan Ponce de León
and His Lands of Discovery

Vasco da Gama
and the Sea Route to India

Explorers of New Lands

Ferdinand Magellan
and the Quest to Circle the Globe

Samuel Willard Crompton

Series Consulting Editor William H. Goetzmann
Jack S. Blanton, Sr. Chair in History and American Studies
University of Texas, Austin

CHELSEA HOUSE
PUBLISHERS
A Haights Cross Communications Company ®
Philadelphia

CHELSEA HOUSE PUBLISHERS
VP, New Product Development Sally Cheney
Director of Production Kim Shinners
Creative Manager Takeshi Takahashi
Manufacturing Manager Diann Grasse

Staff for FERDINAND MAGELLAN
Executive Editor Lee Marcott
Editorial Assistant Carla Greenberg
Production Editor Noelle Nardone
Photo Editor Sarah Bloom
Cover and Interior Designer Keith Trego
Layout 21st Century Publishing and Communications, Inc.

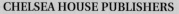

A Haights Cross Communications ❮ Company ®

www.chelseahouse.com

First Printing

9 8 7 6 5 4 3 2 1

Library of Congress Cataloging-in-Publication Data

Crompton, Samuel Willard.
   Ferdinand Magellan and the quest to circle the globe/Samuel Willard Crompton
     p. cm.–(Explorer of new lands)
   Includes bibliographical references and index.
   ISBN 0-7910-8608-9 (hardcover)
   1. Magalhães, Fernão de, d. 1521–Juvenile literature. 2. Explorers–Portugal–Biography–
Juvenile literature. 3. Voyages around the world–Juvenile literature. I Title. II. Series.
G420.M2C76 2005
910.4'1–dc22

                                                                    2005007520

Table of Contents

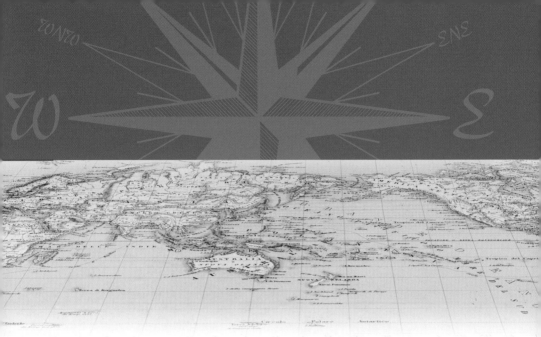

Introduction

by William H. Goetzmann
Jack S. Blanton, Sr. Chair in History and American Studies
University of Texas, Austin

Explorers have always been adventurers. They were, and still are, people of vision and most of all, people of curiosity. The English poet Rudyard Kipling once described the psychology behind the explorer's curiosity:

"Something hidden. Go and find it. Go and
    look behind the Ranges—
Something lost behind the Ranges. Lost and
    waiting for you. Go!" [1]

Miguel de Cervantes, the heroic author of *Don Quixote*, longed to be an explorer-conquistador. So he wrote a personal letter to King Phillip II of Spain asking to be appointed to lead an expedition to the New World. Phillip II turned down his request. Later, while in prison, Cervantes gained revenge. He wrote the immortal story of *Don Quixote*, a broken-down, half-crazy "Knight of La Mancha" who "explored" Spain with his faithful sidekick, Sancho Panza. His was perhaps the first of a long line of revenge novels—a lampoon of the real explorer-conquistadors.

Most of these explorer-conquistadors, such as Columbus and Cortés, are often regarded as heroes who discovered new worlds and empires. They were courageous, brave and clever, but most of them were also cruel to the native peoples they met. For example, Cortés, with a small band of 500 Spanish conquistadors, wiped out the vast

Aztec Empire. He insulted the Aztecs' gods and tore down their temples. A bit later, far down in South America, Francisco Pizarro and Hernando de Soto did the same to the Inca Empire, which was hidden behind a vast upland desert among Peru's towering mountains. Both tasks seem to be impossible, but these conquistadors not only overcame nature and savage armies, they stole their gold and became rich nobles. More astounding, they converted whole countries and even a continent to Spanish Catholicism. Cathedrals replaced blood-soaked temples, and the people of South and Central America, north to the Mexican border, soon spoke only two languages—Portuguese in Brazil and Spanish in the rest of the countries, even extending through the Southwest United States.

Most of the cathedral building and language changing has been attributed to the vast numbers of Spanish and Portuguese missionaries, but trade with and even enslavement of the natives must have played a great part. Also playing an important part were great missions that were half churches and half farming and ranching communities. They offered protection from enemies and a life of stability for the natives. Clearly vast numbers of natives took to these missions. The missions vied with the cruel native caciques, or rulers, for protection and for a constant food supply. We have to ask ourselves: Did the Spanish conquests raise the natives' standard of living? And did a religion of love appeal more to the natives than ones of sheer terror, where hearts were torn out and bodies were tossed down steep temple stairways as sacrifices that were probably eaten by dogs or other wild beasts? These questions are something to think about as you read the Explorers of New Lands series. They are profound questions even today.

"New Lands" does not only refer to the Western Hemisphere and the Spanish/Portuguese conquests there. Our series should probably begin with the fierce Vikings—Eric the Red, who discovered Greenland in 982, and Leif Ericson, who discovered North America in 1002, followed, probably a year later, by a settler named Bjorni. The Viking sagas (or tales passed down through generations) tell the stories of these men and of Fredis, the first woman discoverer of a New Land. She became a savior of the Viking men when, wielding a broadsword and screaming like a madwoman, she single-handedly routed the native Beothuks who were about to wipe out the earliest Viking settlement in North America that can be identified. The Vikings did not, however, last as long in North America as they did in Greenland and Northern England. The natives of the north were far tougher than the natives of the south and the Caribbean.

Far away, on virtually the other side of the world, traders were making their way east toward China. Persians and Arabs as well as Mongols established a trade route to the Far East via such fabled cities as Samarkand, Bukhara, and Kashgar and across the Hindu Kush and Pamir Mountains to Tibet and beyond. One of our volumes tells the story of Marco Polo, who crossed from Byzantium (later Constantinople) overland along the Silk Road to China and the court of Kublai Khan, the Mongol emperor. This was a crossing over wild deserts and towering mountains, as long as Columbus's Atlantic crossing to the Caribbean. His journey came under less dangerous (no pirates yet) and more comfortable conditions than that of the Polos, Nicolo and Maffeo, who from 1260 to 1269 made their way across these endless wastes while making friends, not enemies, of the fierce Mongols. In 1271, they took along Marco Polo (who was Nicolo's son and Maffeo's nephew). Marco became a great favorite of Kublai Khan and stayed in China till 1292. He even became the ruler of one of Kublai Khan's largest cities, Hangchow.

Before he returned, Marco Polo had learned of many of the Chinese ports, and because of Chinese trade to the west across the Indian Ocean, he knew of East Africa as far as Zanzibar. He also knew of the Spice Islands and Japan. When he returned to his home city of Venice he brought enviable new knowledge with him, about gunpowder, paper and paper money, coal, tea making, and the role of worms that create silk! While captured by Genoese forces, he dictated an account of his amazing adventures, which included vast amounts of new information, not only about China, but about the geography of nearly half of the globe. This is one hallmark of great explorers. How much did they contribute to the world's body of knowledge? These earlier inquisitive explorers were important members of a culture of science that stemmed from world trade and genuine curiosity. For the Polos crossing over deserts, mountains and very dangerous tribal-dominated countries or regions, theirs was a hard-won knowledge. As you read about Marco Polo's travels, try and count the many new things and descriptions he brought to Mediterranean countries.

Besides the Polos, however, there were many Islamic traders who traveled to China, like Ibn Battuta, who came from Morocco in Northwest Africa. An Italian Jewish rabbi-trader, Jacob d'Ancona, made his way via India in 1270 to the great Chinese trading port of Zaitun, where he spent much of his time. Both of these explorer-travelers left extensive reports of their expeditions, which rivaled those of the Polos but were less known, as are the neglected accounts of Roman Catholic friars who entered China, one of whom became bishop of Zaitun.[2]

In 1453, the Turkish Empire cut off the Silk Road to Asia. But Turkey was thwarted when, in 1497 and 1498, the Portuguese captain Vasco da Gama sailed from Lisbon around the tip of Africa, up to Arab-controlled Mozambique, and across the

Indian Ocean to Calicut on the western coast of India. He faced the hostility of Arab traders who virtually dominated Calicut. He took care of this problem on a second voyage in 1502 with 20 ships to safeguard the interests of colonists brought to India by another Portuguese captain, Pedro Álvares Cabral. Da Gama laid siege to Calicut and destroyed a fleet of 29 warships. He secured Calicut for the Portuguese settlers and opened a spice route to the islands of the Indies that made Portugal and Spain rich. Spices were valued nearly as much as gold since without refrigeration, foods would spoil. The spices disguised this, and also made the food taste good. Virtually every culture in the world has some kind of stew. Almost all of them depend on spices. Can you name some spices that come from the faraway Spice Islands?

Of course most Americans have heard of Christopher Columbus, who in 1492 sailed west across the Atlantic for the Indies and China. Instead, on four voyages, he reached Hispaniola (now Haiti and the Dominican Republic), Cuba and Jamaica. He created a vision of a New World, populated by what he misleadingly called Indians.

Conquistadors like the Italian sailing for Portugal, Amerigo Vespucci, followed Columbus and in 1502 reached South America at what is now Brazil. His landing there explains Brazil's Portuguese language origins as well as how America got its name on Renaissance charts drawn on vellum or dried sheepskin.

Meanwhile, the English heard of a Portuguese discovery of marvelous fishing grounds off Labrador (discovered by the Vikings and rediscovered by a mysterious freelance Portuguese sailor named the "Labrador"). They sent John Cabot in 1497 to locate these fishing grounds. He found them, and Newfoundland and Labrador as well. It marked the British discovery of North America.

In this first series there are strange tales of other explorers of new lands—Juan Ponce de León, who sought riches and possibly a fountain of youth (everlasting life) and died in Florida; Francisco Coronado, whose men discovered the Grand Canyon and at Zuñi established what became the heart of the Spanish Southwest before the creation of Santa Fe; and de Soto, who after helping to conquer the Incas, boldly ravaged what is now the

American South and Southeast. He also found that the Indian Mound Builder cultures, centered in Cahokia across the Mississippi from present-day St. Louis, had no gold and did not welcome him. Garcilaso de la Vega, the last Inca, lived to write de Soto's story, called *The Florida of the Inca*—a revenge story to match that of Cervantes, who like Garcilaso de la Vega ended up in the tiny Spanish town of Burgos. The two writers never met. Why was this—especially since Cervantes was the tax collector? Perhaps this was when he was in prison writing *Don Quixote.*

In 1513 Vasco Núñez de Balboa discovered the Pacific Ocean "from a peak in Darien"[3] and was soon beheaded by a rival conquistador. But perhaps the greatest Pacific feat was Ferdinand Magellan's voyage around the world from 1519 to 1522, which he did not survive.

Magellan was a Portuguese who sailed for Spain down the Atlantic and through the Strait of Magellan—a narrow passage to the Pacific. He journeyed across that ocean to the Philippines, where he was killed in a fight with the natives. As a recent biography put it, he had "sailed over the edge of the world."[4] His men continued west, and the *Victoria,* the last of his five ships, worn and battered, reached Spain.

Sir Francis Drake, a privateer and lifelong enemy of Spain, sailed for Queen Elizabeth of England on a secret mission in 1577 to find a passage across the Americas for England. Though he sailed, as he put it, "along the backside of Nueva Espanola"[5] as far north as Alaska perhaps, he found no such passage. He then sailed west around the world to England. He survived to help defeat the huge Spanish Armada sent by Phillip II to take England in 1588. Alas he could not give up his bad habit of privateering, and died of dysentery off Porto Bello, Panama. Drake did not find what he was looking for "beyond the ranges," but it wasn't his curiosity that killed him. He may have been the greatest explorer of them all!

While reading our series of great explorers, think about the many questions that arise in your reading, which I hope inspires you to great deeds.

Notes

1. Rudyard Kipling, "The Explorer" (1898). See Jon Heurtl, *Rudyard Kipling: Selected Poems* (New York: Barnes & Noble Books, 2004), 7.

2. Jacob D'Ancona, David Shelbourne, translator, *The City of Light: The Hidden Journal of the Man Who Entered China Four Years Before Marco Polo* (New York: Citadel Press, 1997).

3. John Keats, "On First Looking Into Chapman's Homer."

4. Laurence Bergreen, *Over the Edge of the World: Magellan's Terrifying Circumnavigation of the Globe* (New York: William Morrow & Company, 2003).

5. See Richard Hakluyt, *Principal Navigations, Voyages, Traffiques and Discoveries of the English Nation*; section on Sir Francis Drake.

1

The
Strait

It was the third week of October in the year 1520. Four small ships approached a waterway called a strait. On board were about 200 men, drawn from Spain, Portugal, and other European nations.

In command was Ferdinand Magellan. He was about 40 years old and had spent at least half his life on the seas and oceans of the world. Nothing he had done before was as exciting as this moment. For days and months he had searched. For months and years he had dreamed. Now, at last, he entered the strait that now bears his name. We call it the Strait of Magellan.

If you look at a map of the Western Hemisphere, you see that North, Central, and South America form a remarkable line of land. From Hudson Bay in the north to Tierra del Fuego in the south, there is almost no place where ships can pass through. But the idea of passing through the Americas and reaching China, Japan, or India was a treasured one. Sailor after sailor gave his life seeking the so-called "Northwest Passage." By passing through the solid rock of North, Central, or South America, this sailor hoped to reach the fabled treasures of the eastern lands.

For centuries, no one found the Northwest Passage. Except for brief times when the summer sunshine melts part of the Arctic glaciers, there is no such passage. But there is a Southwest Passage. We don't call it that. We call it the Strait of Magellan in honor of the great explorer. This is his story.

Today people still go through the Strait of Magellan. The different types of land and water forms amaze them. This is still a land little touched by humans. There are mounds of ice, depending on what time of year it is. There are many penguins and other hardy animals that can live in this severe climate. But mostly there is rock, water, and ice.

This was where Magellan entered on October 20, 1520.

It took a lot of faith to enter the strait. Magellan had no satellite to guide him. He didn't even have what we could call a proper compass and navigational equipment. Like all sailors of his day, Magellan relied on his eyes, his ears, the North Star, and the Southern Cross. These were his instruments as he plunged into the strait, taking his four ships and 200 sailors.

Not all of his sailors were pleased. In fact, many were not. But they had learned not to confront Magellan, their captain-general. Magellan had already shown himself to be incredibly tough. He had put down a mutiny using strength and wit. He was a very clever man and also a rather ruthless one.

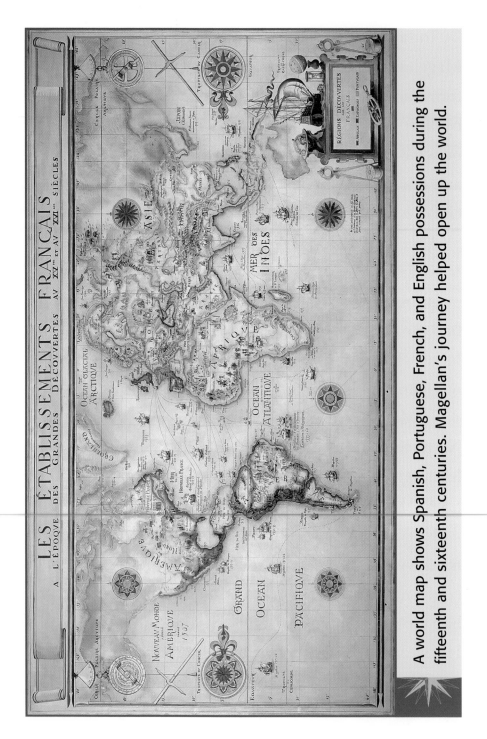

A world map shows Spanish, Portuguese, French, and English possessions during the fifteenth and sixteenth centuries. Magellan's journey helped open up the world.

So in they sailed. The little ships looked like cockleshells as they passed the cliffs and entered the cold and mysterious waterway. Magellan was so happy. His men were so afraid. But they went in anyway. And the world has never been quite the same since.

Test Your Knowledge

1 What is a strait?

   a. A wide placid lake fed by several rivers

   b. A waterfall

   c. A mountain stream that reaches the sea

   d. A waterway connecting two larger
      bodies of water

2 How many men were on Magellan's
expedition?

   a. 50

   b. 100

   c. 200

   d. 12

3 In entering the strait, what was Magellan seeking?

   a. An advantage over his enemies

   b. Shelter from a storm

   c. An all-water route to the Far East

   d. None of the above

4 How experienced a sailor was Magellan?

   a. He was new to ocean sailing but hoped to
      succeed by luck.

   b. He had steered his last ship onto the rocks.

   c. He had spent nearly half his life at sea and
      trusted his instincts.

   d. None of the above.

5 What sort of navigational tools did Magellan rely upon?

a. Satellites and global positioning systems

b. His senses and intuition

c. A compass and sextant

d. None of the above

ANSWERS: 1. d; 2. c; 3. c; 4. c; 5. b

Portugal and Spain

Toward the end of the fifteenth century, Portugal and Spain were the superpowers of Western Europe. We say *superpower* when we refer to a great and powerful nation that has the might to influence its neighbors.

Together, Portugal and Spain occupy the Iberian Peninsula. The Pyrenees Mountains form the northeast border of the peninsula and the Atlantic Ocean is its western border. Part of the Mediterranean Sea forms the southern boundary. All this water around the Iberian Peninsula meant that the people there—the Spanish and the Portuguese—learned a lot about the sea.

Even though Portugal is a small and rather poor country, the Portuguese led the way at first. In the fifteenth century, Prince Henry the Navigator sent one ship out after another. He wanted to find a route to the spices of the Far East, and he believed the best way to do this was to sail around Africa. The problem, of course, was that neither he nor his captains knew much about Africa at all. They had no idea how large its landmass was, or how long it would take to sail around it.

Year after year, Prince Henry the Navigator persisted. He sent out captain after captain on ship after ship. Each captain did his best, but they all came back with the same tales of terror and woe. The sailors were too scared, they said, and there were frightening creatures that lurked in the darkness. Africa was too large, and another route would have to be found. Prince Henry the Navigator died

talent de bienfaire

Prince Henry the Navigator, of Portugal, wanted to find a route to the Far East to obtain spices. He believed that sailing around Africa would be the best route.

long before Portugal solved the riddle of how to get around the African landmass.

The Portuguese did not give up on the quest, though. Even after Prince Henry's death, Portuguese captains kept exploring along the coast of West Africa. Progress took a long time in those days, but by the 1480s, the Portuguese were about to reach the bottom (southern) tip of Africa. King John II of Portugal was very excited about the prospect.

SEEKING OUT SPICES

The golden dream, or perhaps the scented dream, was one of spices. Europeans wanted cinnamon, ginger, pepper, and mace. They wanted these spices, which both preserved food and made it taste better. Europeans had first become accustomed to these tastes during the Crusades, and now there were bold explorers who wanted to find a new way to the source of the spices.

No European had yet been there, but there were about five special islands, halfway across the world, in what is now the Republic of Indonesia. These small islands produced most of the spices that were dried, packaged, and shipped across two continents for Europeans to enjoy. They became known as the Spice Islands.

Portugal was leading in the race. In 1488, Captain Bartholomew Diaz rounded the Cape of Good Hope, at the extreme southern tip of Africa. He was the first European to sail that far and the first to sail into the Indian Ocean. Even though the Spice Islands were a long way off, it seemed certain that Portugal would be the first nation to reach them.

Enter Columbus.

Christopher Columbus appeared at the Portuguese court in the 1480s. He was a poor adventurer, an Italian sailor from the city of Genoa. Columbus had spent much of his life at sea, and he was convinced there was a better way to reach the fabled Spice Islands. Instead of sailing around Africa and to the *east*, he proposed striking straight across the Atlantic by sailing *west*. Since the world was round (Columbus and most sailors believed this), he would surely reach the Spice Islands eventually.

The idea was a good one. But King John did not like Columbus or his idea. King John and Portugal had invested much time and money in the pursuit of the Spice Islands, by the route around Africa. Now, just as they were about to see the triumph of this long-held hope, the Portuguese heard Columbus say they were going in the wrong direction.

King John said no. Columbus went across part of the Iberian Peninsula and approached the king and queen of Spain.

King Ferdinand was not interested, but Queen Isabella was. She listened to Columbus and told him that the time was not ripe. He should wait until she and her husband had defeated the Moors, who lived in the southern part of the Iberian Peninsula.

Columbus waited. And waited. A few years passed. He was just about to give up entirely and leave for France, or some other country, when a horseman came to tell him the queen was ready. She and King Ferdinand had won their war against the Moors.

Columbus went to the royal palace. Because he had waited so long and because he had endured so much poverty while waiting, he was very arrogant in his demands. He wanted to be called "Admiral of the Ocean Sea," and he wanted a 10 percent royalty on all profits that would come from his voyage (this royalty was to be passed onto his children after him).

King Ferdinand was ready to tell the foreign adventurer to go away, but Queen Isabella was prepared to take the chance. She pawned some of her jewels to finance the expedition, which set sail from the port town of Palos in August 1492.

Everyone knows what happened next. After two months of frightening travel, Columbus and his three ships hailed land in what is now the Bahamas. They were the first Europeans to cross the Atlantic and claim part of the New World for their nation (the Vikings had crossed around the year 1000, but they had not claimed or settled the land).

HAILED AS THE GREATEST

Two great events had taken place. Bartholomew Diaz had rounded the Cape of Good Hope and become the first European to sail into the Indian Ocean. Columbus had sailed west and found land, which, he thought, was part of India or China. That is why he called the people he met "Indians."

News traveled back to Europe rather quickly this time. Columbus arrived home in 1493. He was hailed as the greatest explorer of his time. Meanwhile, Bartholomew Diaz had returned to Portugal, where *he* was hailed as the greatest.

Portugal and Spain not only ruled the Iberian Peninsula. Their ships now threatened to take over other parts of the world. This was a wonderful thing for Portugal and Spain, but not for the natives they would conquer. Nor would it be good if Portuguese and Spanish sailors fought each other as they claimed far-off lands.

Enter the pope.

Alexander VI was a Spaniard by birth. He became pope in 1492, the same year that Columbus crossed the Atlantic Ocean. Portugal and Spain approached Pope Alexander. Each nation asked him to do something about the possible conflicts that might arise between them.

In 1493, Pope Alexander VI announced his decision. He would prevent future trouble between the two powers that ruled the Iberian Peninsula. Pope Alexander asked for, and received, the best maps and globes of the time. He drew a line down the middle of each one, and declared that in the future, all the lands discovered to the west of this line would belong to Spain, and all the lands to its east would belong to Portugal. That was that.

The future, it appeared, would belong to the two superpowers of the Iberian Peninsula.

The Papacy

The papacy was one of the great powers of the fifteenth and sixteenth centuries. Popes did not have large armies or domains, but they had great influence over their fellow rulers and the peoples of all Christian nations.

Rodrigo Borgia was a Spaniard. He became Pope Alexander VI in 1492 and was one of the first of what we call the "Renaissance Popes." Fascinated by art, music, and beautiful things, Pope Alexander VI commissioned great works of art for Rome as a whole and for the Vatican in particular. He also scandalized the Catholic Church by having a mistress and several illegitimate children; one of them was Cesare Borgia, considered one of the most dangerous men at the turn of the sixteenth century.

Alexander VI was followed by Pope Julius II in 1503. Julius was even more enthusiastic about art, money, and worldly power than Alexander

There was a need, however, for new explorers. Christopher Columbus and Bartholomew Diaz had already done their best work for Spain and Portugal. Who would come next?

had been. Pope Julius fought a series of wars to expand the size of the Papal States. He also commissioned Michelangelo to paint the ceiling of the Sistine Chapel in Rome. Though a lot of people, then and now, disapprove of many of Pope Julius's actions, his decision to hire Michelangelo turned out to be one of the great success stories of the age. The Sistine Chapel is one of the greatest draws in Rome for tourists and pilgrims alike.

Pope Julius II died in 1513 and was followed by Pope Leo X. A member of the House of Medici, he is believed to have said, "Now that God has given us the papacy, let us enjoy it." Pope Leo continued the trend of high spending for artistic and architectural projects. These expenditures contributed to the breakup of the Roman Catholic Church in the 1520s, the separation between Catholics and Protestants.

Ferdinand Magellan devoted his life, his fortunes, and his honor to the mission of trying to circle the globe.

In the northwest corner of Portugal, a teenager prepared for what he hoped would be his great future. He was Ferdinand Magellan, and his work would eventually bring together parts of the Portuguese dream and the Spanish one.

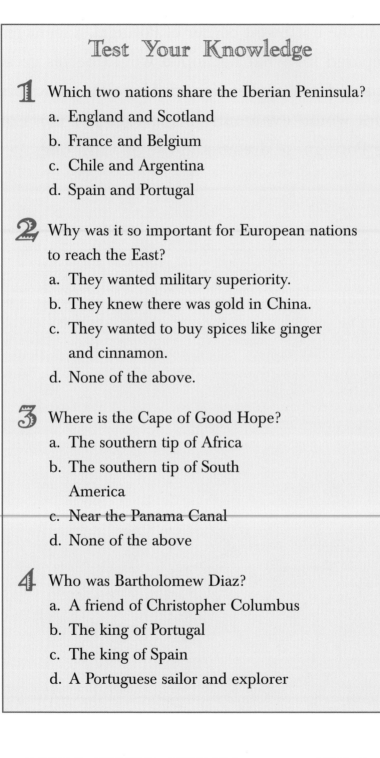

Test Your Knowledge

1 Which two nations share the Iberian Peninsula?
  a. England and Scotland
  b. France and Belgium
  c. Chile and Argentina
  d. Spain and Portugal

2 Why was it so important for European nations to reach the East?
  a. They wanted military superiority.
  b. They knew there was gold in China.
  c. They wanted to buy spices like ginger and cinnamon.
  d. None of the above.

3 Where is the Cape of Good Hope?
  a. The southern tip of Africa
  b. The southern tip of South America
  c. Near the Panama Canal
  d. None of the above

4 Who was Bartholomew Diaz?
  a. A friend of Christopher Columbus
  b. The king of Portugal
  c. The king of Spain
  d. A Portuguese sailor and explorer

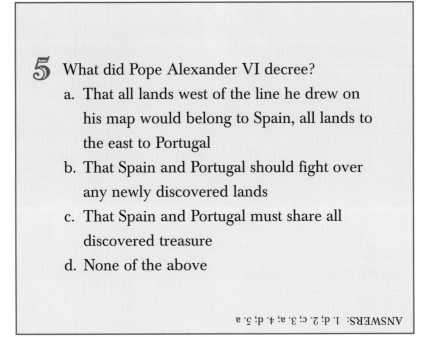

5 What did Pope Alexander VI decree?

a. That all lands west of the line he drew on his map would belong to Spain, all lands to the east to Portugal

b. That Spain and Portugal should fight over any newly discovered lands

c. That Spain and Portugal must share all discovered treasure

d. None of the above

Magellan in the Indian Ocean

Ferdinand Magellan is one of the greatest explorers in all of world history. Surprisingly, we know much more about what he did on his voyages than about his early life. Much of his early life remains a mystery to us today.

Ferdinand Magellan was born around the year 1480, in Sabrosa in northwest Portugal. His father was a member of the fourth order of the Portuguese nobility, and the family was descended from a French knight who had come to Portugal in the eleventh century. The Magellans had probably stayed on their land in northwest Portugal since that time.

We know very little about Magellan's early family life. There is a story that the family lived in a two-story home, and that the first floor was used to house the farm animals. If so, this shows that being a member of the fourth order of nobility meant no special privileges. There is also the possibility that Magellan's mother was a Jew who converted to Catholicism. Even so, we have no proof. Certainly Magellan would carry himself like a proud Christian throughout his life.

Conversions from Judaism to Christianity were common in Portugal at that time. The king of Portugal, like King Ferdinand and Queen Isabella in Spain, wanted his kingdom to be 100 percent Roman Catholic. Many people were forced to convert to

Christianity. Some others did so willingly. Others left the kingdom and went to foreign lands.

Around the age of 12, Magellan and his brother Diego went to Lisbon. They were accepted as pages at the household of Queen Eleanor of Portugal. The work was not hard, but it went on all day long. Magellan and his brother learned to bow, move gracefully, dance, and the like. They probably learned the art of telling jokes for the amusement of the royal family. But there may have been other, more substantial, tasks. Because Portugal was a maritime nation, with men and ships always at sea, Magellan may have learned about the globe, the atlas, and the compass. All this took place before he ever went to sea.

Magellan had his heart set on an ocean voyage, but he was bitterly disappointed by the events of 1495. King John II died and was succeeded by King Manuel I. King Manuel seemed to have taken a dislike to Magellan from the start. Perhaps it was because Magellan had served the previous king. In any case, King Manuel I did not allow Magellan or his brother to go on Vasco da Gama's important voyage.

Earlier, we saw that Bartholomew Diaz was the first European to "round" (go around) the Cape of Good Hope. He had not gone much farther, though. Now, in 1497 and 1498, another Portuguese expedition, led by Vasco da Gama, rounded the cape and sailed through the Indian Ocean, all the way to the western coast of India. How Magellan must have envied the lucky sailors who were able to go on this great voyage. Portugal had found a new route to the Indies.

YEARNING FOR THE SEA

Years passed. Magellan and his brother remained at court. They each had a small salary from the king, but no adventure and no chance to make their lives more interesting. The two brothers longed to go to sea.

Finally, in 1505, Magellan and his brother were allowed to join a very large expedition. It sailed from Portugal that summer and reached the coast of India late that autumn. We do not know much about how Magellan enjoyed his first great sea voyage, but we can guess that he thrilled to it. This was exciting, to sail down to the southern part of the Atlantic and then across the Indian Ocean.

We know more about Magellan once he reached India. The Portuguese were setting up forts and trading posts on the Indian coast. Naturally this provoked the people who were already there conducting trade. One such group consisted of Arab merchants, who had been in the Indian Ocean for hundreds of years. Another group consisted of Venetian merchants. Venice had not found the route to India that Portugal had, but Venice had another route. The Venetian merchants and sailors could go to Egypt, pass overland a little while, and then use the Red Sea to reach the Indian Ocean.

As you might expect, battles arose between the Portuguese on one side and the Arabs and the Venetians on the other. Some of the battles were very savage, and the Portuguese almost always won in the end. Magellan fought with distinction in these battles. On one occasion, he was the only officer to insist that his ship go back to rescue a group of stranded sailors. Even now, with limited experience, Magellan had a great feel for men, ships, and the sea.

Magellan spent the next five years in the Indies. This was the name for all the lands and waters of

Gondolas pass the Rialto Bridge in Venice, Italy. In the fifteenth century, Venetian merchants traded with India by sailing to Egypt, traveling overland, and then sailing on the Red Sea to the Indian Ocean. When the Portuguese found a new route to India, conflicts arose between the Venetians and the Portuguese.

the Indian Ocean. His goal, though, and that of most other Portuguese sailors, was to reach the fabled Spice Islands.

Today we know a lot more about those islands. Five in number, they are now called the Moluccan Islands. These islands have a special combination of wind, water, rain and overall weather that allow spices of all kinds to grow there. The native people learned to cultivate these spices and to sell them to people in far-off lands. India received most of the spices, and Indian merchants then sold them to Arabs, Venetians, and others. This was why there was such a competition for who was to rule the Indian Ocean.

The Spice Islands

There are places in the world that seem destined for certain things. The countries on the Iberian Peninsula appeared destined to thrive at sea because they bordered on the Atlantic, the Mediterranean, and the Bay of Biscay. The Spice Islands, in far-off Indonesia, appeared destined to produce nutmeg, cinnamon, ginger, and pepper for the rest of the world.

There are five Spice Islands: Ternate, Tidore, Motir, Makian, and Bacan. The first two, Ternate and Tidore, are known for the height of their mountains, which reach as much as 6,500 feet above sea level even though the islands are only about 40 square miles in size.

There is a special combination of moisture, warmth, and rain in the Spice Islands, and this

Magellan wanted to reach the Spice Islands, but he was not the first to do so. His good friend Francisco Serrao led three Portuguese ships from Sumatra sometime in 1511. Serrao stumbled around a bit, but he found the Spice Islands, and became the first European ever to arrive there.

combination allows them to produce the fabulous spices that drew Ferdinand Magellan and many others. The Europeans depended on the Spice Islands for a long time, but then they learned how to grow and cultivate those plants in other locations. The Spice Islands began to lose their importance.

Many types of food around the world are now transplanted and grown in other locations. Some, though, defy the attempt of humans to do this. Oranges and bananas still have to be grown in a certain type of climate. As long as humans are around, we can be sure there will be more attempts to transplant animals, foods, plants, and the like. Man does not leave his environment the way he found it.

A special combination of moisture and warmth allows spices, like nutmeg, above, to flourish on the Spice Islands. Cinnamon, ginger, and pepper are also prevalent.

Within a short time of his arrival, Serrao made friends with the ruler of the island of Ternate. Serrao married one of the ruler's daughters and settled down to a wonderfully comfortable life as a grand vizier and chief consultant.

Magellan was not on this voyage, but he learned about it. He received several letters from Serrao, describing the beauty of the islands and the ease of life there. Magellan wanted to follow his friend to the Spice Islands, but duty ruled otherwise. Magellan was ordered to return to Portugal in 1511.

Like a good sailor and soldier, Magellan followed his orders. He traveled back across the great Indian Ocean, rounded the Cape of Good Hope, and sailed home. But he took with him a Malay Islander whom he gave the Christian name of Enrique. This man became Magellan's slave, friend, and personal protector. They would be together for the rest of Magellan's life.

Once he arrived home, Magellan found that his pockets were empty. He had not gained any treasure while in the Indian Ocean, and he was as poor as when he had started. This was not true for some of his fellows. The lucky ones had concentrated on obtaining spices or silver or gold. Not so Magellan. He had concentrated on exploration and the hope of glory.

A NEW MISSION

A poor nobleman needed money, and Magellan signed on for a new adventure. In 1513, King Manuel I sent a large fleet and army to the west coast of Africa to subdue a rebellion against Portuguese rule. This was going to be hard fighting in a tough, hot climate, but Magellan went anyway.

Like any nobleman, Magellan had to have a horse for the expedition. He bought one at a low price, leading some of his fellow nobles to ridicule him. How could he bear to ride such a poor-looking horse, they wondered. This was bad for Magellan, who was always concerned about his dignity. Maybe this was because he was shorter than average or because he had grown up rather poor. In any case, Magellan was always quick to respond to slights.

The horse was killed in a battle with the native people. Magellan asked for the full price of such a warhorse to be sent to him, but the treasurer only gave him a little money, pointing out that his horse had not been a great animal in the first place. If this was not bad enough, Magellan then suffered a harsh wound in his leg, from a lance thrust by an Arab horseman. Magellan would limp for the rest of his life.

SNUBBED BY THE KING

Some men would have given up. Magellan was tired, wounded, and angry, but he never gave up. Instead he sailed home to Portugal and asked for a meeting with King Manuel I. The king agreed, and Magellan asked him to pay for the horse and to increase the small salary paid to him as a member of the royal household.

Not surprisingly, the king refused.

Worse yet, he sent Magellan all the way back to the coast of Africa to have him tried by his fellow officers for abandoning the army without leave. Magellan went all that way and was found not guilty in the trial.

Again, Magellan returned to Portugal. He went to the king one more time, asking for an increase in his small salary. When the king refused, Magellan told him that he had a special plan to increase the fortune of Portugal and to help himself as well. He wanted to lead a group of ships in the direction that Christopher Columbus had sailed all those years ago. He wanted to reach the Spice Islands of the east by sailing west.

King Manuel was not stupid. He probably knew there was something good to this plan. But if he was going to send an expedition this way, he could find someone better than Ferdinand Magellan to lead it. Or so he thought, anyway. The king refused.

Magellan was frustrated. He was angry. He was furious.

The king had blocked his way time and time again. But Magellan knew he could not show his anger toward the king. Therefore he asked King Manuel I if he might offer his services to some other leader in the Christian world. Manuel answered scornfully that Magellan could go wherever he liked.

Courtesy required that Magellan step forward, kneel, and kiss the king's hands. This was hard to do, since the king had made life so difficult for him so many times. But Magellan stepped forward and sank to his knees.

The king stuck his hands underneath his royal robes. He turned his head away, showing that he would not let Magellan offer his final gesture.

Humiliated beyond belief, Magellan turned to go. As he limped away from the throne, some of the courtiers laughed and made fun of his limp.

This was the last time Magellan would be in his homeland. It was also the last chance Portugal would ever have to claim the services of its brilliant but difficult nobleman.

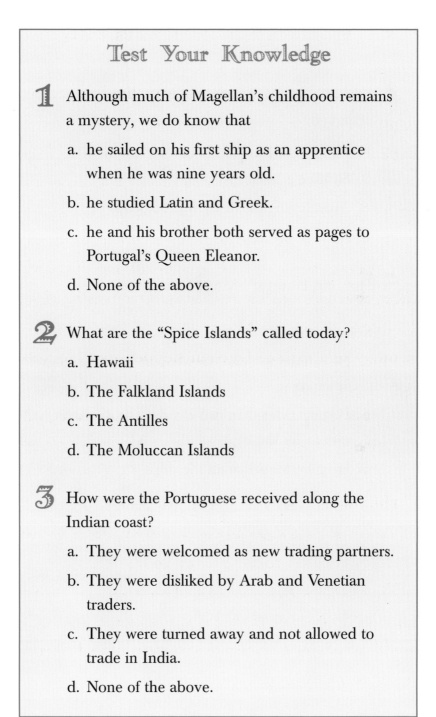

Test Your Knowledge

1 Although much of Magellan's childhood remains a mystery, we do know that

   a. he sailed on his first ship as an apprentice when he was nine years old.

   b. he studied Latin and Greek.

   c. he and his brother both served as pages to Portugal's Queen Eleanor.

   d. None of the above.

2 What are the "Spice Islands" called today?

   a. Hawaii

   b. The Falkland Islands

   c. The Antilles

   d. The Moluccan Islands

3 How were the Portuguese received along the Indian coast?

   a. They were welcomed as new trading partners.

   b. They were disliked by Arab and Venetian traders.

   c. They were turned away and not allowed to trade in India.

   d. None of the above.

4. For what offense was Magellan tried and later acquitted?

   a. Mutiny

   b. Stealing a horse

   c. Abandoning the army without leave

   d. None of the above

5. How did Portugal's King Manuel respond to Magellan's idea to seek a western route to the Spice Islands?

   a. He refused to give Magellan any money, ships, or supplies.

   b. He gave Magellan two old ships and meager rations for the trip.

   c. He gave Magellan all the ships, supplies, and money he requested.

   d. None of the above.

ANSWERS: 1. c; 2. d; 3. b; 4. c; 5. a

The King
of Spain

Magellan left Portugal in a hurry. He headed for Spain. These two countries were in serious competition with each other. They each wanted the wealth of the Spice Islands.

The two countries were also very involved with each other. The first wife of King Manuel I of Portugal was a

Spanish princess. She died young, and his second wife was also a Spanish princess. She had died recently, and he was now planning to marry Princess Eleanor, the older sister of King Charles of Spain.

So, because of the family connections, it was important for Portugal and Spain to stay on friendly terms. But beneath the surface, both King Manuel of Portugal and King Charles of Spain wanted to outdo each other.

Magellan arrived in the city of Seville in October 1517. He came in the company of an astrologer named Faleiro. This man believed in Magellan's idea of sailing west to reach the Spice Islands of the east.

Around the same time that Magellan arrived in Seville, King Charles arrived in Spain.

Born in Belgium in 1500, King Charles was only 17 years old. He had been raised at the Belgian court (it was called Burgundy in those days), and he had never seen Spain before. But he was the eldest grandson of King Ferdinand and Queen Isabella, and it made sense that he would be the new king of Spain.

King Charles of Spain appears here in a portrait from later in his life. When Magellan met with Charles in 1518, the new king was 18 years old. He was greatly impressed with Magellan's plan to find a new way to the Spice Islands.

King Charles and his Belgian courtiers landed in northern Spain and headed south toward the court city of Valladolid. Magellan stayed in Seville because he had made new friends. One of them was his future wife.

We don't know very much about Beatriz Barbosa. She was the daughter of a Portuguese man who had moved to Spain a few years earlier. Magellan stayed at the family's home and courted their daughter. Magellan and Beatriz married before the year was over.

Not only did she make him a home and provide him with an important father-in-law, but Beatriz also brought a dowry to Magellan. At that time it was believed that a woman or girl should bring something of value to her husband. Her family money came to something like $80,000 today.

Magellan now had some things for which he had waited a lifetime. He could have stayed in Seville, as a happily married man, and could have enjoyed a comfortable life. This was something he had never had before. But Magellan's ambition called to him. He still wanted to sail west in order to reach the east.

AN AUDIENCE WITH KING CHARLES

So, in the early part of 1518, Magellan and Faleiro

went to the Spanish court at Valladolid. They asked for an audience with King Charles.

To get to see the king, Magellan and Faleiro had to make a deal with a leading nobleman at court. He demanded 10 percent of all the profits they might make, just in order to arrange a meeting with the king. These delays and outlays infuriated Magellan, but he had no choice. As a Portuguese in Spain, he was now rather a man without a country. He had to play by whatever rules men like this nobleman set.

Magellan and Faleiro had their audience in March 1518. This was a scene and a moment that has been captured by many artists and writers since. It was a great moment in the history of world exploration.

King Charles had just turned 18. Like most young men he was filled with ambition and hope. He had more reason to believe that his hopes would be realized than most young men, and he was very excited by Magellan's idea.

The basic idea was the same that Christopher Columbus had first proposed to King Ferdinand and Queen Isabella: reach the Far East by sailing to the west. But Magellan was up against an obstacle that Columbus had not faced. Columbus had not known that there was an immense body of land–North, Central, and South America–in between Europe and the coast of Asia. King Charles did know this, because of the explorations of men like Columbus and Vasco Núñez de Balboa,

Geography in the Time of Magellan

Geography was improving, but it did so very slowly. Just a few generations earlier, in the time before Christopher Columbus's great voyage, many people believed that the Earth was flat and that ships would fall off if they went too far. This idea was largely gone by the time of Magellan.

Still, there were a lot of questions. How big around was the Earth? How long would it take to sail all the way around the world? How big, for that matter, was Asia?

No one really knew. The best estimates were made by men who studied the writings of Marco Polo, the geographer Ptolemy, and others. Most of them believed, accurately, that the Earth was round, but most of them also underestimated how who had recently become the first Spaniard to see the Pacific Ocean (Balboa climbed a palm tree on the Isthmus of Panama and saw the distant blue water).

Magellan had an answer to this problem. He had talked with many Portuguese sailors and mapmakers before leaving Portugal. Magellan was sure

far it was around. Today we know the Earth is about 24,900 miles around at the equator. In the time of Magellan, most geographers thought it was about 16,000 miles.

Subtracting 16,000 from 24,900, we see that the geographers underestimated by about 8,900 miles. That's an immense distance, more than twice the breadth of the United States.

Given that they underestimated the circumference of the Earth, the geographers tended to agree with Ferdinand Magellan. He thought that he would find the strait that led from the Atlantic Ocean to the Pacific, and that from there it would be a rather short sail to reach Asia.

How far off were they? We will see in Chapter 8.

that there was a strait—a narrow waterway between two large bodies of water—that would lead through South America and come out on the other side.

How could he be so sure? No one had seen this strait. But Magellan knew that a recent Portuguese expedition had found a major body of water (what is now the Río de la Plata), and he believed this water would lead him to the Pacific Ocean.

So far so good. But what about Portugal?

Magellan had an answer for that, too. He brought forth his Malay slave Enrique, who now spoke Spanish. Enrique told the Spanish king that the Spice Islands lay within the Spanish side of the line drawn down the world by Pope Alexander VI. How did Enrique know?

Well, he had been to the Spice Islands. But Enrique was a slave. How could his word be taken on such an important matter?

Magellan then pulled out his trump card, letters from his friend Francisco Serrao. Serrao was living in the Spice Islands. He had sent letters to Magellan, telling him how wonderful the islands were, and assuring him that they were in the Spanish zone of control.

Did Magellan make the letters up? Did he make them sound more promising than they really were? No one will ever know.

We do know that King Charles was impressed. He loved the idea of finding a new way to the Spice Islands. He wanted to best the king of Portugal. King Charles decided in favor of the expedition on that very day. His court officials drew up a contract that gave Magellan a lot of what he wanted, though not all.

Magellan and Faleiro were to have a 10-year monopoly on trade with the lands they found. No other Spanish ships or crews would be sent to the Spice Islands, and Magellan and Faleiro would be able to set up trade in the way they wanted.

What was more, King Charles would provide five ships. They would sail from the port of Seville.

Having received almost all he had sought, Magellan was thrilled. He and King Charles seemed to understand each other. Leaving Faleiro in Valladolid, Magellan went quickly to Seville.

DISAPPOINTMENT AND PREPARATIONS

What he found disappointed him. Five ships were

provided, over the next few months. But they were old and unseaworthy. It would take months of work to get them ready for a major voyage.

Magellan was used to disappointment, even to hardship. He went about the difficult work of fixing the ships and finding crew members. The second part was even harder than the first, since word had spread around Seville that Magellan was something of a madman.

Was there any truth to this? Yes, if you count determination as madness. It had taken a certain mad determination for Magellan to get this far, and he was not about to stop. So even though the task was very challenging, he found and recruited sailors.

They came from all over Europe. There were many Spaniards and Portuguese, to be sure, but there were also Irish, French, and English sailors. There were even two citizens from the island of Rhodes in the eastern Mediterranean. By the time the voyage was over, their island would fall to the Ottoman Turks in a terrible siege that caught the attention of all of Christian Europe.

There was also an Italian, from Lombardy to be precise. Antonio Pigafetta was 26 or 27 years old.

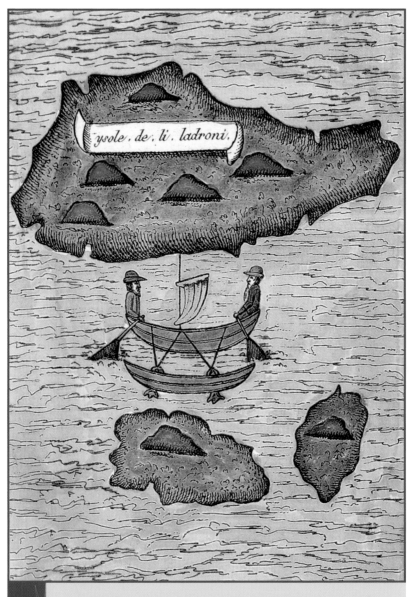

ysole. de. li. ladroni.

Above is a page from *The First Voyage Around the World* by Antonio Pigafetta. A minor diplomat who went on Magellan's expedition, Pigafetta became one of its best diarists and record-keepers.

He had served the papal bureaucracy for the last few years and had come to Spain as a minor diplomat. Meeting Magellan and learning about the expedition, Pigafetta asked his superiors to be allowed to go on the voyage. They agreed, and Pigafetta became one of the best diarists and record-keepers of the next three years.

By the summer of 1519, Magellan had his crew members, his ships, and most of his captains. There were about 250 men in all, lodged aboard the five ships. But he had no choice when it came to the top officer class. Spain was determined that Magellan, as a Portuguese, should not take too many Portuguese officers. Therefore it was decided that he had to have a large number of Spanish officers.

Most of these men were fine, and Magellan did not have any problem with them. But a few of the very top officers proved difficult from the beginning. One of them, Captain Juan de Cartagena, was an important Spanish nobleman. He made it clear that he resented serving under a Portuguese leader. Cartagena was going to be trouble, but Magellan had no choice. It was either sail with Cartagena or give up the voyage entirely.

Knowing Magellan, there was only one possible answer. He would go forward, no matter the obstacles.

AN EXPLORER'S WILL

As the day of departure grew near, Magellan drew up his will. He provided for his wife, his infant son, and the child who was as yet unborn. There were also provisions for his Portuguese relatives and for several churches and convents. One of the most touching provisions, though, is as follows:

> I declare and ordain as free and quit of every obligation of captivity, subjection, and slavery, my captured slave Enrique, mulatto, native of the city of Molucca . . . and I desire that of my estate there may be given to the said Enrique the sum of ten thousand maravedis in money for his support.[1]

Certainly one can ask: Why did Magellan not free him on the spot? Even so, it was a rare owner or master who provided 10,000 maravedis for a former slave.

On August 10, 1519, the five ships slipped their moorings and headed down the Guadalquivir River, headed for the open sea. Even though this was only the first step of their long journey, it was one of the most dangerous. There was a terrible sandbar at the mouth of the Guadalquivir River, and many Spanish ships had wrecked there over the years. Luckily, all five ships of the little fleet got past the bar and reached the open sea.

They were on their way!

Test Your Knowledge

1 How did Magellan's marriage to Beatriz Barbosa benefit him?

   a. Beatriz provided Magellan with a stable home.

   b. Magellan gained an influential father-in-law.

   c. Beatriz brought a dowry that today would value $80,000.

   d. All of the above.

2 How did Magellan persuade young King Charles to support his expedition?

   a. He assured the king that he could capture the islands from the Portuguese.

   b. He assured the king that a strait would let him pass from the Atlantic to the Pacific.

   c. He promised the king half of any riches he found along the way.

   d. None of the above.

3 What did King Charles promise Magellan?

   a. A fleet of 20 seaworthy ships

   b. A 10-year monopoly on trading rights with the Spice Islands

   c. All the provisions and weapons he would need

   d. None of the above

4 What delayed the start of Magellan's expedition?

a. Bad weather

b. Insufficient funds

c. The ships King Charles provided were old and needed repairs

d. None of the above

5 Before departing, Magellan drew up a will that provided

a. money for his wife, son, and unborn child.

b. money for his Portuguese relatives and several churches.

c. freedom and a sizable amount of money for his servant Enrique.

d. All of the above.

ANSWERS: 1. d; 2. b; 3. b; 4. c; 5. d

Magellan in
the Atlantic

Five little ships sailed from the mouth of the Guadalquivir River. The *Trinidad* (which was Magellan's flagship), *Concepcion*, *Victoria*, *Santiago*, and *San Antonio* sailed into the broad Atlantic Ocean.

For the first few weeks, the crew members saw familiar sights. Some of them had come this way before, edging down the west coast of Africa. Portuguese and Spanish ships made this trip rather regularly.

Then the winds changed a bit. They started blowing in a southeasterly direction, and the sailors expected to set out across the Atlantic. To their surprise, Ferdinand Magellan insisted that the ships continue south near the African coast.

Magellan was never very good at telling his captains "why." He made all the big decisions himself and usually kept his reasons to himself, too. But he had a good reason for making this move. He had learned that Portugal was out to get him.

Magellan was truly a man without a country. He had only been a Spanish citizen for two years, and many Spaniards distrusted him. The situation was even worse in Portugal, where his name was now that of a traitor's. King Manuel I had been furious to learn that Spain had accepted Magellan's idea and given him a fleet. The Magellan coat of arms, standing outside the little house in northwest Portugal, had been defaced.

Worse, King Manuel I sent ships to patrol the eastern Atlantic Ocean. He expected that Magellan would sail straight across the Atlantic and that his

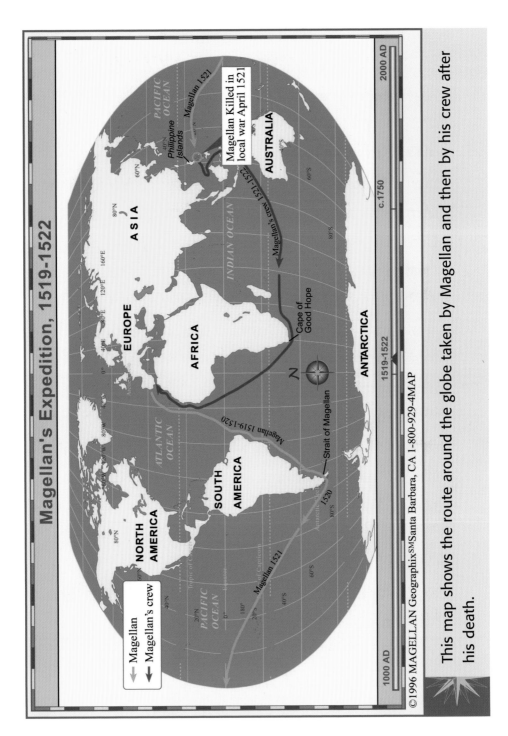

Magellan's Expedition, 1519-1522

This map shows the route around the globe taken by Magellan and then by his crew after his death.

patrol ships would capture him. Knowing this, Magellan wisely stuck to the coast of Africa for longer than his sailors thought proper.

A CONFRONTATION

Juan de Cartagena became furious because Magellan did not give him directions in advance. Instead, Magellan required that each captain come along-side the flagship each night and ask for the next day's sailing directions. Angry over this, Captain Cartagena showed increasing disrespect for Magellan, sometimes calling him "captain" rather than "captain-general."

Tensions came to a head as doldrums delayed the fleet. These are areas where the winds are very light, not strong enough to propel even the small ships of Magellan's fleet.

A passionate conversation took place one night in Magellan's cabin aboard the flagship. Captain Cartagena demanded, as in the past, that Magellan give him the full sailing instructions for the entire voyage. He would not wait for each day to unfold.

Suddenly Magellan stood up and drew his knife. Placing it under Cartagena's neck, he hissed,

"Rebel, this is mutiny!"[2] Cartagena appealed to the other captains sitting in the cabin, begging that they turn on Magellan. They did not, and Captain Cartagena spent some time over the next few days on deck in a pillory with his head and hands held in stocks.

Some of the other captains thought this was shameful to do to a Spanish nobleman. They complained, and Magellan allowed Captain Cartagena to be released into the custody of the captain of the *Trinidad*. Even so, Magellan had clearly shown that he, and no one else, was the leader of the fleet.

Now the fleet turned westward. The ships escaped from the doldrums and made their way across the southern Atlantic. Only a week passed before the crews sighted the landmass of South America. One major part of their voyage had passed.

REACHING SOUTH AMERICA

Magellan led his crews and ships into the Bay of the River of January (its name today is Rio de Janeiro, the most famous city in Brazil). Portuguese explorers had known this area for over 15 years, and Magellan knew he would find fresh food and water here. What

Today, the city of Rio de Janeiro sprawls along the coast of Brazil. When Magellan and his crew landed there, Portuguese explorers had only known the area for 15 years. The natives were quite friendly to the crew.

he did not count on was the friendliness of the native people, especially the women.

Hundreds of natives came out to greet the sailors. Some paddled out in canoes, and others swam out on their own power. In either case, the natives were very curious about the Europeans. Many of them, women especially, came on board the ships and showed their friendliness toward the sailors. For the average sailor, who had weathered the coast of Africa, the doldrums, and then the Atlantic, this was a wonderful time.

The natives provided different types of foods. They also tried to steal items from the ships, but Magellan and his other captains were very watchful. Generally, Magellan was less concerned about what the natives might steal than about the ability of his men to resist the charms of the people and the place. A few men did desert, but most were corralled back onto the ships. With some regret, the sailors manned the ships and left the River of January after just a few weeks.

The five little ships sailed due south and arrived at the mouth of the Río de la Plata, in what is now Argentina. This was the body of water Magellan expected would carry him to the Pacific Ocean, but just a few days of exploration showed that this was not the case. The water of the Río de la Plata became fresh as the ships sailed west, and it soon became obvious that the river, while a major body of water, was not a true strait between the Atlantic and Pacific Oceans.

Magellan was disappointed, but he turned the ships south and edged along the east coast of South America. He was determined to find his strait.

Over the next few weeks the sailors became alarmed. They could see that Magellan was taking them farther and farther south and that the weather

Portugal and Brazil

As we saw in Chapter 2, Pope Alexander VI drew a line down the center of the world, at least the center of the world that the Europeans knew. Pope Alexander declared that everything found to the west of this line would belong to Spain, and everything to its east would belong to Portugal. Naturally this brings up the question: How did Portugal wind up with Brazil?

The answers lie in geography and diplomacy. The South American continent bulges out to the east far more than one expects until one examines the map carefully. This is because the eastern part of South America and the western part of Africa were once joined together millions of years ago. When they split apart, as part of the was changing. As you sail south from the equator the seasonal patterns are reversed, so that what is spring in the Northern Hemisphere is autumn in the Southern Hemisphere. Magellan and his men were headed right into this weather pattern, and they were frightened.

continental drift patterns, South America was left with a great bulge pointed toward Africa. This bulge went over the line drawn by Pope Alexander VI and meant that Brazil fell within the Portuguese part of the world.

The second answer, or reason, belongs to diplomacy. Even though Pope Alexander drew the line in 1493, there were endless redrawings, treaties, and arguments about the matter. The issue was only settled in the time of Pope Julius II. He was not a Spaniard, as Pope Alexander had been, and he was inclined to treat the two countries with an even hand. The result was that Brazil fell within the Portuguese side of the treaty line, and the Brazilians of today, at least most of them, speak Portuguese.

People muttered about mutiny, about getting rid of this terrible captain-general. But few men actually dared to do anything. Magellan wore a suit of armor at all times, and his Malay slave Enrique guarded him day and night. Even though the captain-general was a small man, there was something quite scary about his manner and ways. Few men really wanted to tangle with him.

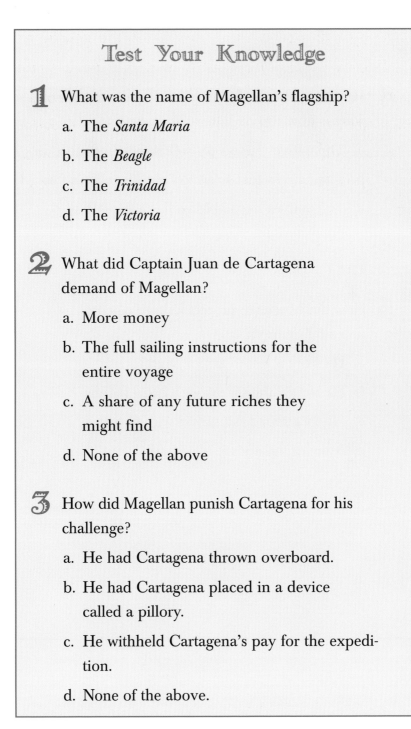

Test Your Knowledge

1 What was the name of Magellan's flagship?

  a. The *Santa Maria*

  b. The *Beagle*

  c. The *Trinidad*

  d. The *Victoria*

2 What did Captain Juan de Cartagena demand of Magellan?

  a. More money

  b. The full sailing instructions for the entire voyage

  c. A share of any future riches they might find

  d. None of the above

3 How did Magellan punish Cartagena for his challenge?

  a. He had Cartagena thrown overboard.

  b. He had Cartagena placed in a device called a pillory.

  c. He withheld Cartagena's pay for the expedition.

  d. None of the above.

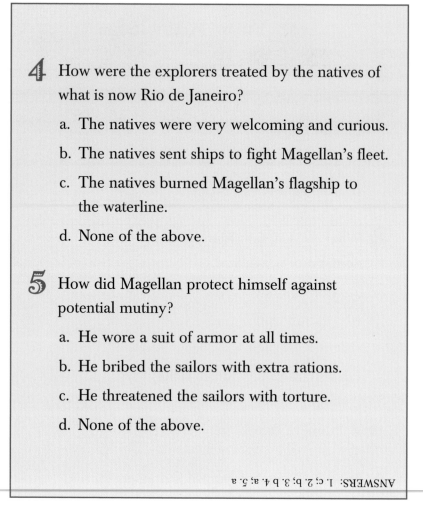

4 How were the explorers treated by the natives of what is now Rio de Janeiro?

   a. The natives were very welcoming and curious.

   b. The natives sent ships to fight Magellan's fleet.

   c. The natives burned Magellan's flagship to the waterline.

   d. None of the above.

5 How did Magellan protect himself against potential mutiny?

   a. He wore a suit of armor at all times.

   b. He bribed the sailors with extra rations.

   c. He threatened the sailors with torture.

   d. None of the above.

ANSWERS: 1. c; 2. b; 3. b; 4. a; 5. a

Mutiny!

Juan de Cartagena had a plan. He had not forgiven
Magellan for placing him under arrest while the
fleet was off the African coast. Then again, he had not
forgiven Magellan, a Portuguese, for having been given
command of the fleet in the first place. Juan de Cartagena
was out to get Ferdinand Magellan.

While the ships were anchored in the mouth of San Julian Harbor in what is now Patagonia, Cartagena sprang his trap. Magellan was caught unawares.

Many of the sailors were desperate. They saw the weather turning against them, and they knew that their captain-general would never turn back. Magellan's steely determination worked against him in this case, since some crewmen who might have stayed loyal now joined the mutiny.

All five ships were anchored at Port San Julian. The date was April 1, 1520, Easter Sunday. Magellan went around his flagship, the *Trinidad,* talking to the crewmen and making sure they were loyal to him. To one of his friends he confided that he knew that three captains intended to murder him when he went ashore to celebrate Easter Mass.

Despite this knowledge, Magellan went ahead and took part in the Mass. Three of the other captains stayed on their ships, ignoring Magellan and the ceremony. One other captain came ashore, but he declined Magellan's request to dine with him. From that alone, Magellan judged that at least three ships and three captains were against him.

This ship is a replica of one used by Ferdinand Magellan on his voyage. He began the expedition with five ships. Three ships rebelled against Magellan at Port San Julian.

During that evening, three ships anchored closer to shore became part of a full-fledged mutiny. Juan de Cartagena was one of the leaders. Another was Juan Sebastian Elcano, a Basque sailor. The mutineers intended to kill Magellan or at least keep him in irons until they returned to Spain.

Magellan knew how serious the situation was. One other ship, commanded by a Spaniard with no loyalty to either side, remained neutral. Other than that, it was Magellan, leading the *Trinidad,* against three shiploads of mutineers.

QUELLING THE REBELLION

Magellan acted on the morning of April 2. He sent a boat to the *San Antonio,* claiming he wished to discuss a way out of the situation. The way was found when the captain of the *San Antonio* refused even to discuss the matter. Two men who had brought the message pulled out their knives and killed him on the spot. A second boatload of Magellan's loyal sailors attacked the *San Antonio* just minutes later. The mutinous crew hardly resisted. They were too stunned by the death of their captain.

Now it was two ships against two, with one other remaining neutral. No! The captain of the "neutral" ship now joined Magellan, making it three loyal ships to two that were still mutinous.

That night Magellan had every reason to celebrate. He had turned the tables on his enemies. The fact that they were anchored closer to shore than

Ferdinand Magellan made sure he avenged the thwarted mutiny against him. He marooned a ship captain and a priest, and executed two other men.

he was turned out to be a weakness on their part. Magellan could sail in to get them or he could sail away, at his choice. But they were trapped inside San Julian Harbor.

During the night of April 2, Magellan sent some of his men in a boat to cut the moorings of one of the mutinous ships. They succeeded, and the ship drifted helplessly down the harbor. When the ship came within range, Magellan opened fire. His men

Medieval Punishments

Magellan was certainly harsh toward the mutineers among his crew. But his methods were typical of the time.

Nearly all European nations followed something called Roman Law, which came from the ancient Roman Empire. The trials and methods of punishment were often barbaric by today's standards.

An accused person was not considered innocent until proven guilty. Rather, he was expected to prove his innocence. Very few jury trials were held. Most decisions were made by a judge, who often found it convenient to support the government or the social system rather than the swarmed over the sides, and soon they captured the next-to-the-last of the mutineers.

All it took the next day was for Magellan to sail alongside the last of the five ships. Juan de Cartagena and the last of the mutineers surrendered without a fight. Magellan had come back into his own. The fleet was all his, once again.

Magellan was furious at Captain Cartagena, and with good reason. Cartagena had tried several times

person who was accused. Of course there were good judges and there were courts that did the best they could for the defendant, but on the whole, this was a tough system if you were the person accused.

Finally came the punishments: hanging, strangulation, drawing-and-quartering. All of these were what we now call cruel and unusual punishments, but they were standard in Magellan's day.

We have to remember that this was a world where a person could lose a hand for stealing a loaf of bread. Europeans believed it was necessary to strike at those found guilty with all their might, and they usually succeeded.

to sabotage the expedition. Magellan could have had him killed, but knowing that he was a major nobleman in Spain, it made better sense to maroon him. Magellan announced that Cartagena and a priest who had worked together in the mutiny would be stranded on an island when the fleet left the area. Two other men were executed on the spot.

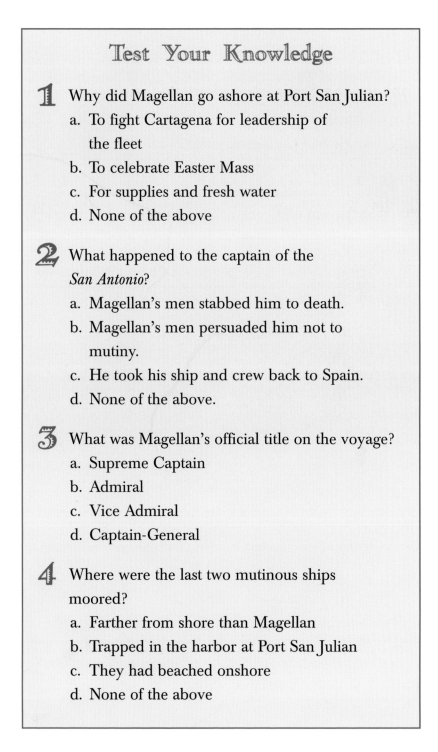

Test Your Knowledge

1 Why did Magellan go ashore at Port San Julian?
a. To fight Cartagena for leadership of the fleet
b. To celebrate Easter Mass
c. For supplies and fresh water
d. None of the above

2 What happened to the captain of the *San Antonio*?
a. Magellan's men stabbed him to death.
b. Magellan's men persuaded him not to mutiny.
c. He took his ship and crew back to Spain.
d. None of the above.

3 What was Magellan's official title on the voyage?
a. Supreme Captain
b. Admiral
c. Vice Admiral
d. Captain-General

4 Where were the last two mutinous ships moored?
a. Farther from shore than Magellan
b. Trapped in the harbor at Port San Julian
c. They had beached onshore
d. None of the above

5 How did Magellan punish the mutinous Captain Cartagena?

a. He had Cartagena publicly hanged.

b. He threw Cartagena to the sharks.

c. He marooned Cartagena on an island.

d. He cut off Cartagena's right thumb.

ANSWERS: 1. b; 2. a; 3. d; 4. b; 5. c

At the Bottom of the World

Magellan and his sailors stayed in San Julian Harbor until August. This was not a good time for the men, who feared that their captain-general would lead them to even worse dangers than before. But now that the mutiny was behind them, the men stayed quiet. Some even said that Magellan had magical powers, which had brought him and them this far.

Magellan learned that there was another channel of water about 60 miles south of San Julian Harbor. He sent Captain Juan Rodriguez Serrano and the *Santiago* south to investigate. Magellan truly appreciated Captain Serrano, who had stayed loyal to him during the mutiny. Serrano's mission was to explore this body of water to see if it was the strait, and to look for fresh sources of food.

Disaster struck. Captain Serrano brought the *Santiago* into the Santa Cruz estuary where it was caught on a series of reefs. The little ship broke up in a matter of minutes after the men escaped. They jumped to boats and into the water, and most of them made it to shore.

They were on the south side of the estuary, however, a very bad spot since they were even farther from help. Captain Serrano and his men built rafts, which got a handful of men across the estuary. They then walked through 60 miles or more of perilous country of which they knew virtually nothing. The men made it to San Julian Harbor, but they looked more dead than alive when they arrived.

Magellan acted quickly. Food and supplies were sent by land, and the stranded men were rescued. Once again, Magellan demonstrated his quick-thinking, quick-acting ways. He saved the men and some of the materials from the little ship, but the fleet that had sailed from Spain was now reduced from five ships to four.

THE LAST OF A MUTINEER

In September 1520, Magellan and his men sailed from Port San Julian. This had been their home for several months, but the men were not sorry to leave. The memory of the mutiny was fresh in their minds, as were the punishments Magellan had meted out. His final act was to maroon Captain Juan de Cartagena and a rebellious priest on a little island. Magellan had them sent ashore with a good supply of food and wine, but no one doubted that this would be the last of Cartagena, who had made so much trouble for the captain-general. Now it was time to sail south.

The four little ships sailed south into fierce winds and sudden gusts. Nothing they had ever done before had prepared them for sailing in the South

Atlantic. But Magellan drove them on. He had to find the strait that would lead from the South Atlantic to the South Pacific.

On October 20, 1520, about a month out of Port San Julian, the ships found the entrance to what looked like a strait. Unlike the previous bodies of water, which had all been disappointments, this one was wide enough to indicate that it might lead to the Pacific. Magellan had one of his men put ashore. The man went up the highest rock he could find and reported back that there was water leading steadily to the west. It looked as if this would be the real thing.

Today we know much more about this area than Magellan did. We know that this area, now called the Strait of Magellan, is one of the most beautiful and most haunting places in the world. Rocks come right down to the edge of the water, sometimes making sheer cliffs. The water itself is a mixture of blue and gray, and no one wants to swim in it: It is far too cold. The cold temperatures are created by the glaciers, some of which look blue, that edge over the landscape. This was, and is, one of the most forbidding areas anywhere on the globe.

Today, the occasional oil rig dots the Strait of Magellan in Chile, South America. Another mutiny arose on one of Magellan's four ships while it was exploring the strait, and the rebels took the ship back to Spain.

Magellan sailed in. He had always been like that. Danger did not stop him.

The spirits of his men picked up, too. At least there was now a chance they might get away from the fierce Atlantic Ocean.

EXPLORING THE STRAIT

Magellan sent two of his four ships ahead, to investigate what the channel and body of water was like. He and the other two ships stayed back, collecting fresh food. The sailors found plenty of fish and some seals as well.

Days passed. Magellan became very worried. He *must* not lose contact with those two ships! But just as his fears reached their greatest, the two ships appeared with all hands on deck and the men firing their cannons in pleasure. They came to report that the way was clear. No, they had not seen the Pacific Ocean. They did not even know how far it might be. But they found saltwater wherever they went, indicating that this was a genuine strait and not another disappointment.

Magellan ordered all four ships to go forward. His spirits soared, and those of his sailors were good enough. The little ships sailed west-by-southwest.

There were two places where the channel, or strait, narrowed considerably. The ships had to edge their way past cliffs, and the sailors looked up in amazement at the gray and blue ice that sheeted the rocks above. But they made it through these narrow parts, and before long came to a great island in the middle of the strait: today it is called Dawson Island.

Magellan did not know, could not know, which way to go around. So he ordered two ships to sail on the eastern side of the island and he led the other two ships on the western side. The expedition broke into two parts yet again.

Magellan and his two ships, on the western side, explored a good way. They then returned to the top (northern) part of the island and waited to meet the other two ships.

A SHIP IS LOST

Disaster struck yet again.

Only one of the two ships returned. The *San Antonio*, the largest ship in the fleet, was nowhere to be found.

Magellan spent days looking for the *San Antonio*. He and his men sailed the eastern side of the island time and again, searching for the lost ship. Finally, almost in despair, Magellan asked his astronomer, who was also an astrologer, to cast a horoscope to see what had happened to the *San Antonio*.

The Crew of the *San Antonio*

The astronomer-astrologer had been right. Magellan's cousin, Captain Mesquita, was in chains, and the *San Antonio* was heading back to Spain.

While the *San Antonio* investigated the eastern side of Dawson Island, a mutiny took place. Magellan's cousin was stabbed, removed from command, and put in chains. The crew, led by the experienced pilot Gomes, turned the ship around and headed for Spain. Given that theirs was a mission of exploration, and that Magellan was their captain-general, this was mutiny and treason, punishable by the worst form of torture and death.

When the *San Antonio* arrived in Spain, the crew members, led by Gomes, told a lot of lies about Magellan. There was some truth behind the accusations, but many lies as well. As a result,

Andres de San Martin, the astronomer-astrologer, looked at the stars and gave Magellan very bad news. His cousin, who had been placed in command of the *San Antonio*, had been arrested and was in chains. The ship itself had left the Strait of Magellan and was in the Atlantic Ocean.

Magellan's wife and son were placed in custody, and Magellan would have to stand trial when he returned to Spain.

Most dangerous was the anger of Bishop Fonseca, leader of the Spanish bureaucracy that governed the business of exploration. He was almost certainly the father of Juan de Cartagena and when he learned that his illegitimate son had been marooned, his anger knew no bounds. If Magellan eventually made it home, he had better bring plenty of spice, silk, and treasure to make up for what he had done wrong so far.

Most unfair, Captain Mesquita was thrown in jail. He, the legitimate captain, suffered imprisonment, while the mutineers went free. If there were any justice in the Spanish world, it would have to wait until Magellan returned.

Magellan did not know whether to believe this or not. He did know, however, that he had to get through the strait. He could wait no longer. So, early in November, the fleet, which was now reduced to three ships, began to head on the western side of the island, following a channel that led west-by-northwest.

Once they left the area around Dawson Island, Magellan and his men saw the waters change. The channel was narrower than before, but it was promising because it continued to be saltwater and because of the direction in which it led. Magellan and his three little ships sailed west, and found that the channel required constant monitoring. There were rocks, reefs, and sandbars aplenty. Only a very careful sailor could make it through these waters.

Days passed. Then one of Magellan's sailors, sent to a rocky outcrop, reported that he saw clear water in all directions. The Pacific!

The ships sailed on, but the sailors found they had been deceived. The waters had opened considerably for a way, but then they closed up again. Night after night Magellan's men heard the pounding of waves on breakers. They knew the sea was

This sixteenth-century map of the Strait of Magellan is from the expedition of Admiral George Spilbergen. Rocks, reefs, and sandbars made sailing through the strait treacherous.

not far off, but they were not certain whether that sea might pound them into bits, as had happened to the *Santiago* in the Santa Cruz estuary.

On November 28, 1520, the crewmen of the ship *Victoria* sighted a cape on their port (left) bow. They gave it two names: Beautiful and Desired. Once they passed this cape they were in the open sea, the Pacific Ocean that they had sought for so long.

We don't know what Magellan's first reaction was. But knowing the type of man he was and the strength of his religious belief, we are inclined to think he sank to his knees and thanked God and the Virgin Mary for bringing him and three of his five ships to this point. He had entered the Pacific Ocean, and he believed that the Spice Islands were not very far away.

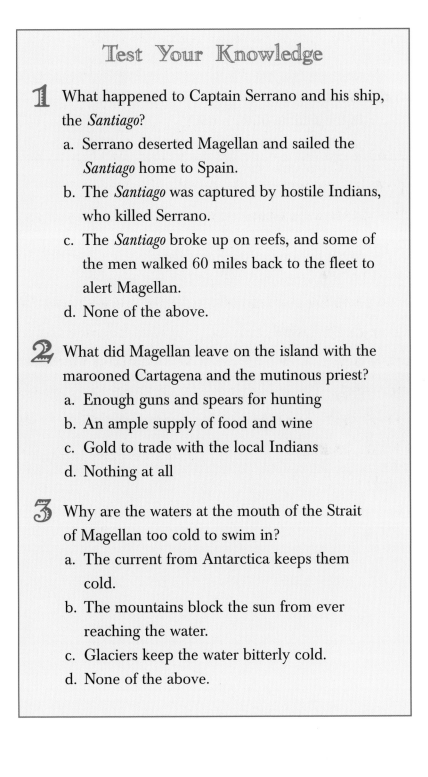

Test Your Knowledge

1 What happened to Captain Serrano and his ship, the *Santiago*?

   a. Serrano deserted Magellan and sailed the *Santiago* home to Spain.

   b. The *Santiago* was captured by hostile Indians, who killed Serrano.

   c. The *Santiago* broke up on reefs, and some of the men walked 60 miles back to the fleet to alert Magellan.

   d. None of the above.

2 What did Magellan leave on the island with the marooned Cartagena and the mutinous priest?

   a. Enough guns and spears for hunting

   b. An ample supply of food and wine

   c. Gold to trade with the local Indians

   d. Nothing at all

3 Why are the waters at the mouth of the Strait of Magellan too cold to swim in?

   a. The current from Antarctica keeps them cold.

   b. The mountains block the sun from ever reaching the water.

   c. Glaciers keep the water bitterly cold.

   d. None of the above.

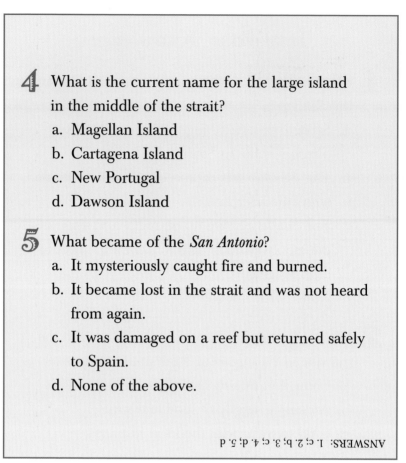

4 What is the current name for the large island in the middle of the strait?

a. Magellan Island

b. Cartagena Island

c. New Portugal

d. Dawson Island

5 What became of the *San Antonio*?

a. It mysteriously caught fire and burned.

b. It became lost in the strait and was not heard from again.

c. It was damaged on a reef but returned safely to Spain.

d. None of the above.

ANSWERS: 1. c; 2. b; 3. c; 4. d; 5. d

Magellan in
the Pacific Ocean

Magellan was the first European to name it. He called it *Mar Pacifico* (Pacific Ocean) because the waters seem very peaceful (pacific) when he first saw them as he came out of the Strait of Magellan.

Many sailors from our times would question this decision. The Pacific Ocean is anything but calm.

True, there are some places and some times when the Pacific seems gentle. But these are almost always the calm before the storm.

We have already seen that the Atlantic Ocean was rough in many parts. But the Atlantic, strong as it is, gets its water from fewer sources than the Pacific does. The Pacific is the largest ocean in the world. It draws water from as far off as China and the Philippines on one side and the Andes and the rivers of Guatemala on the other.

This was the great ocean that Magellan now entered.

At first he sailed up the west coast of South America. As he sailed north, he and his crewmen were able to get fresh food and water from the coastal areas. But there were few natives, and almost none of them were friendly. So Magellan decided to strike out across the Pacific.

The Juan Fernandez Islands lie well off the coast of South America. Magellan sailed between these islands and the mainland, but he did not take on enough food from either place. Truly, Magellan was about to make his greatest mistake.

This portrait of Magellan appeared in the fables of La Fontaine. After coming though the Strait of Magellan, the expedition sailed up the western coast of South America, where the crewmen could get fresh food and water.

A CRUCIAL MISCALCULATION

Magellan's sense of geography was based on that of Ptolemy, who had written during the first century A.D. Ptolemy had understated the size of the Earth, thinking it was about 16,000 miles around instead of 24,900. This major difference meant that Magellan thought the Pacific would be a short ocean to cross and that he would soon be in the Spice Islands of Indonesia. He would see his old friend and comrade Francisco Serrao.

The three little ships headed west, across the Pacific.

For some time they saw no islands at all. No land to be seen. This was witnessed much later, in the twentieth century, when men first went into space and looked back at Earth. If they happened to be looking at the Pacific, they would ask: Where's the land? There doesn't seem to be any if you are in the southeastern Pacific Ocean.

Magellan sailed by dead reckoning. This meant that he and his sailors used ropes and knots, dangled in the water, to reckon their speed. If the ship was going 10 knots per hour, then he could gauge how far he went each day. Sailors can still use this method today, but they have much more sophisticated methods, like the Global Positioning System (GPS), refined compasses, and radar. Even so, it is still dangerous to sail the vast Pacific. Imagine how dangerous it was in the time of Magellan!

The error of thinking that the world was only 16,000 miles around soon became apparent. Day after day the ships traveled farther to the west, and still they saw no land. Magellan would not hear of turning back, and many of the sailors now agreed with him. They had no wish to thread their way through the treacherous Strait of Magellan a second time.

Morale aboard the ships was high until the fresh food and water began to give out. As bad as things had been before this, there had always been fresh water. Now, with no land in sight, the ships continued on, and the crew members began to drink very brackish water.

RATS FOR DINNER

Food became alarmingly low, and crew members had to give up any ideas of proper behavior when eating. Crewmen ate rats regularly, and some of the diarists commented that even those rats cost half a ducat apiece.

The worst problem was scurvy, which is a disease that strikes when people are low in vitamin C. Scurvy eats away at the skin, and the teeth begin to rot and fall out. The pain from this type of dental disease can only be imagined. The one "barber-surgeon" for the fleet spent most of his time extracting teeth.

A long time, about 250 years, would pass before a solution to scurvy was found. In the eighteenth century, British captains would see that having a lot of limes on board prevented scurvy. The rich lime juice kept scurvy away, and British sailors became known as "limeys." But this was a long time off.

One of the strongest descriptions of the plight of the crew members comes from Antonio Pigafetta, the Italian nobleman who had joined the expedition. He wrote:

> We ate biscuit which was no longer biscuit, but powder of biscuits swarming with worms, for they had eaten the good. It stank strongly of rats' urine. We drank yellow water that had been putrid for many days.[3]

Worse was still to come. When the food was gone, the sailors "ate certain ox hides that covered the tops of the yards to keep them from chafing the shrouds, and which had become exceedingly hard because of the sun, rain, and wind. We soaked them in the sea for four or five days, and then placed them briefly on hot ashes, and so ate them; often we ate sawdust."[4]

Magellan remained rather healthy. Nearly 20 crew members died on the three ships, but he never became sick during the crossing of the Pacific. Neither did Antonio Pigafetta, but he explained that the reason was that he had overcome any fussiness he had ever had about what to eat or drink.

(continued on page 98)

First Contacts

Magellan and his men met the islanders of Guam after 80 days of travel in which they saw no other humans. This kind of sudden and dramatic meeting was typical of what happened in the Age of Discovery.

Whether it was Columbus meeting the people of Hispaniola, or Cortés meeting the Aztecs of Mexico, European explorers would encounter peoples they had never seen before. And the meeting, or contact, would be full of excitement as well as danger.

Because the Europeans left written records, we have a better idea of what they thought than what the natives did. But there is a commonality to many of the first encounters, and we can describe a "typical" first meeting between natives and Europeans.

Usually, the natives were both excited and frightened by the Europeans. They were excited to see people with such different faces and body color, and they were frightened by the European weapons, guns especially.

The Europeans usually looked to the natives for what they could provide them. The Europeans were looking for information about food, water, silver, and gold. The natives did not always oblige. Sometimes they pointed in far-off directions, and said, "Go there," meaning "anywhere but here."

One thing that tended to upset or even ruin first meetings was the concept of property. Europeans considered property to be private, even sacred to some degree. Most of the natives they met thought that this idea was ridiculous and that people should share and share alike. As a result, there were many scrapes and fights.

After an arduous 80-day journey across the Pacific Ocean, Magellan and his ships finally spotted land in what would be Guam, above. While crossing the Pacific, the expedition ran out of fresh water, and many sailors suffered scurvy.

(continued from page 95)

FINALLY, LAND

Magellan still expected to see the Spice Islands at any time. He led the expedition north to the equator and then roughly northwest across the Pacific. Finally, on February 28, 1521, after about 80 days at sea without fresh food or water, the sailors spotted two islands. This was the first land they had seen since South America.

The islands are what we now call Guam and Rota. They played an important part in the Pacific campaigns of World War II, and Guam is still a United States territorial possession today.

Magellan was thrilled to see land. He was ready to send men ashore when canoes carrying many islanders came streaming out to meet the ships.

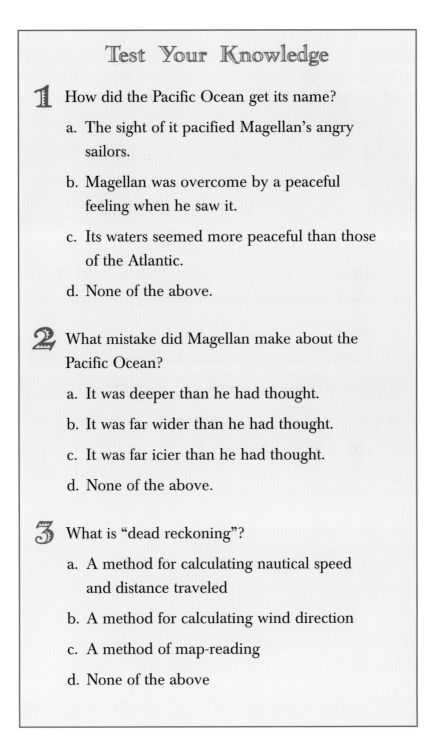

Test Your Knowledge

1 How did the Pacific Ocean get its name?

a. The sight of it pacified Magellan's angry sailors.

b. Magellan was overcome by a peaceful feeling when he saw it.

c. Its waters seemed more peaceful than those of the Atlantic.

d. None of the above.

2 What mistake did Magellan make about the Pacific Ocean?

a. It was deeper than he had thought.

b. It was far wider than he had thought.

c. It was far icier than he had thought.

d. None of the above.

3 What is "dead reckoning"?

a. A method for calculating nautical speed and distance traveled

b. A method for calculating wind direction

c. A method of map-reading

d. None of the above

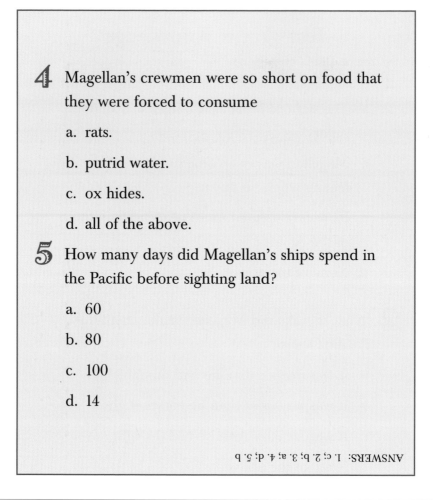

4 Magellan's crewmen were so short on food that they were forced to consume

a. rats.

b. putrid water.

c. ox hides.

d. all of the above.

5 How many days did Magellan's ships spend in the Pacific before sighting land?

a. 60

b. 80

c. 100

d. 14

Tragedy in the Philippines

Magellan had reached land. He was glad. His sailors were even happier. Their captain-general had brought them across the great Pacific Ocean.

The islanders of Guam were happy for a little while. But they had a different idea of what property meant. They stole one of the longboats that belonged to the flagship.

Almost certainly, Magellan would have been better off to have let this go. He was in a very distant land, and his men were hungry and thirsty. But his fierce determination, which was such an advantage when facing the sea, turned into a disadvantage when dealing with people. Magellan could never let anything go.

Therefore, he landed with his men and attacked the villagers. He killed quite a few of them and took the longboat back. But as he returned to his ships, Magellan must have known he could not remain there, near Guam. He had made enemies of its people.

So, after getting some fresh food and water, the expedition sailed west.

Magellan believed he was close to the Spice Islands. As it turns out, he was still more than 1,000 miles away. But he did sail in the right direction, heading west.

Rather than the Spice Islands, Magellan made landfall on the Philippine Islands. He arrived there in March 1521.

UNDERSTANDING THE FILIPINOS

As he and his men exchanged words with the first

Philippine Islanders they met, Magellan was astonished to see that his Malay slave Enrique could understand the words that the Filipinos spoke. Magellan had hoped for this, of course, but so much time had passed that he had almost forgotten about it. Enrique could understand what the Filipinos said, and good communication was established. Not only did this help Magellan and the expedition, but it suggests that Enrique may have been the first person ever to make it completely around the world. He had been in the Malay Peninsula when he became Magellan's slave, and he had crossed the Indian Ocean on his way to Portugal. Then he had sailed from Spain with Magellan, crossed the Atlantic, went through the Strait of Magellan and now the Pacific. Quite possibly, Enrique was the first human ever to accomplish the act of circumnavigation, going completely around the Earth.

Magellan sailed in the eastern part of the Philippine Islands. Around the end of March 1521 he made an alliance with a Philippine chieftain named Humabon. This chief controlled a large section of land and knew the islands and the islanders very well. Magellan seized upon this alliance as a way of making the Philippines part of the growing Spanish Empire.

Of course this was a very bold, perhaps even a foolish, thing to do. King Charles and Spain were very far away. Also, Magellan's task was to find the Spice Islands, not to acquire other lands for Spain. But something happened to Magellan's usually good judgment. He seems to have been carried away with dreams of great power.

Until this point, Magellan had been very much the captain-general of a naval enterprise. Once he landed in the Philippines and tried to work his will there, he became more like a soldier on a wild and daring mission. The whole enterprise started to go to his head.

On March 31, which was Easter Sunday, Magellan went ashore to attend Mass. The ceremony impressed his new Indian allies, and they asked Magellan more about God, Jesus Christ, and the whole set of Christian beliefs. Magellan was only too happy to tell them about Christianity. He was a deeply religious man, who had had little chance to show his faith over the years. He seems to have had

Remnants of the original sixteenth-century cross erected by Ferdinand Magellan are contained in this hollow cross in Cebu City, Philippines. Scenes of Magellan putting up the cross are painted on the dome.

a special feeling for the Virgin Mary, believing that she protected him and the fleet on their mission.

BAPTIZING THE NATIVES

On April 14, which was a Sunday, Magellan went ashore dressed entirely in white. He did so to show the natives his pure intentions. Magellan had a great cross set up, and he proceeded to baptize Chief Humabon and about 800 other Filipinos that day. The baptism continued over the next week and eventually reached about 2,000 people.

There was also an attempt at "faith healing." A very sick man lived in one of the villages controlled by Chief Humabon. Magellan visited this man and gave him some quince preserves. Magellan's store of quince may well be why he did not get scurvy during the long Pacific crossing.

Treasure Ships and Their Routes

Magellan was the first European to cross the Pacific Ocean. In the decades that followed, many other Spaniards and some Portuguese did so, too. They crossed the great ocean to bring treasure to Central America, from where it could go to Spain.

Treasure from the Philippines followed an extraordinarily long route. Galleons were loaded in Philippine ports before crossing the Pacific. Over the decades and centuries that followed, the Spanish pilots found an excellent route. They sailed well north as well as east, intending to see the shore of what is now Oregon. When they saw

Maybe it was the quince, maybe it was the attention he received, but the sick man recovered in a few days. Magellan became even more of a hero to the Philippine Islanders he had met.

As everyone knows, pride comes before a fall.

Magellan was now very full of himself. Having found the strait, crossed the Pacific, and baptized many islanders, he felt he was invincible. Soon he told Chief Humabon that he would fight any and all of the chief's enemies for him.

Cape Blanco (White Cape), they turned south, headed for Acapulco, Mexico.

If all went well, the treasure was unloaded either in Acapulco or in Panama and brought by horse or mule to the eastern side of Central America. There it was reloaded one more time, for the journey to Spain.

As mentioned in Chapter 4, there is an especially dangerous spot just off the mouth of Spain's Guadalquivir River. Many Spanish ships came to grief on this sandbar, and treasure that had come all the way from the Philippines sank within a few miles of its destination.

There may have been some reason behind the boast. Magellan wanted to make Chief Humabon the greatest leader on the Philippine Islands, so that he and King Charles would have a strong, permanent ally there. But the Magellan of one year earlier, even of six months earlier, would not have made such a promise.

Chief Humabon was delighted. He told Magellan about a rival chief named Lapu-Lapu, who lived on a nearby island. Magellan solemnly swore to bring down Chief Lapu-Lapu.

THE DEADLY BATTLE

The Battle for Mactan Island took place on April 27, 1521. Magellan and his men had only been in the Philippines for six weeks, and they were already trying to dominate the area.

Magellan led his men ashore in a pounding surf. He and his fellow Europeans were shocked to see that Chief Humabon and his warriors had not followed. The islanders stayed well offshore, waiting to see how Magellan would handle Chief Lapu-Lapu and his fighters.

Never doubting, at least never seeming to doubt, Magellan went straight ashore. He was greeted with

This picture shows a statue of Lapu-Lapu, the chief of the Mactan tribe in the Philippines. Magellan was killed in 1521 in a battle with Lapu-Lapu.

a wave of arrows, but his body armor protected him. Magellan was joined by a handful of his sailors and soldiers, and they were soon attacked by a much larger number of men, drawn from the island of Mactan.

Antonio Pigafetta, the Italian nobleman, described Magellan's last moments:

> Then, trying to land his hand on his sword, he could draw it out but halfway, because he had been wounded in the arm by a bamboo spear. When the natives saw that, they all hurled themselves upon him. One of them wounded him on the left leg with a large cutlass, which resembles a scimitar, only larger. That caused the captain-general to fall face downward, when immediately they rushed upon him with iron and bamboo spears, and with their bolos until they killed our mirror, our light, our comfort, and our true guide.[5]

Most of the other Europeans had escaped. Magellan died almost alone on the beach.

Test Your Knowledge

1 After leaving Guam, where did Magellan land next?

a. The Spice Islands

b. The Philippines

c. China

d. None of the above

2 Who was Humabon?

a. A Philippine chief friendly to Magellan

b. A Philippine chief hostile to Magellan

c. Magellan's slave

d. None of the above

3 How did the Philippine Islanders initially receive Christianity?

a. They were hostile to any beliefs outside their own.

b. They were curious, and many even agreed to be baptized.

c. They blended Christianity into their own tribal religion.

d. None of the above.

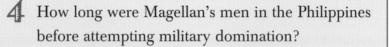 How long were Magellan's men in the Philippines before attempting military domination?

a. A week

b. A month

c. A year

d. Six weeks

5 How did Magellan die?

a. He contracted malaria.

b. He caught a stomach infection from spoiled food.

c. He was killed by natives during a brutal battle on Mactan Island.

d. He took his own life rather than be captured by the natives.

Magellan
and History

Magellan was dead. The mirror, light, comfort, and guide of the expedition was dead. Would the expedition continue? Or might the Europeans join with the Philippine Islanders and slowly blend in with their ways?

Some sailors and soldiers thought it would be better to stay with these islanders. Here, in the Philippines, fruit grew on trees and food was readily available. Even so, these men were overruled by those who wanted to find the Spice Islands. The idea of cinnamon, ginger, and nutmeg overrode the desire for comfort and ease.

BETRAYED

Before they could leave, however, the expedition members suffered another tragedy.

The day after Magellan was killed, one of the ship captains demanded that Enrique, Magellan's slave, go ashore to interpret for the expedition. Enrique refused, saying that he was now a free man. This was true, as we know from Magellan's will. But the captain did not believe, or would not accept, this fact, and he forced Enrique to go ashore and interpret for him with Chief Humabon. Enrique did as he was told.

Three days later, on the first of May, about 30 expedition members went ashore to have a banquet with Chief Humabon. They knew this was the last time they would see this island and its people, so they went determined to enjoy themselves.

The crew members and officers who remained on the ship heard some terrifying shrieks and cries. Then Captain Serrano, who had gone ashore, appeared on the beach, begging for mercy. Several Philippine Islanders were holding him. Serrano shouted across the water that Enrique had betrayed them and that Chief Humabon's warriors had attacked and killed all the others. Serrano begged for the crewmen to barter with the Filipinos to save his life, but it was to no avail. The three ships sailed away from the island, and Serrano perished, along with the other 29 men who had gone ashore.

Enrique was never heard from again.

There was still one more disaster. Shortly after leaving the group of islands where Magellan and 30 other crew members died, the expedition lost another ship. The *Concepcion* was so rotten below the waterline that its crew was rescued and brought onto the two remaining ships: the *Trinidad* and the *Victoria.* The *Concepcion* was then set afire, and it burned and disappeared.

To say things were bad was a great understatement. Originally there had been five ships and

260 men. Now there were two ships and less than 100 men. But the goal, the prize of the Spice Islands, still beckoned.

If the crew members and captains had known the right direction, they might have reached the Spice Islands very quickly. But they did not, and months were spent floundering about in the western islands of the Philippines. At one point the ships were headed in exactly the wrong direction, pointed toward the coast of China. But the captains managed to pick up some islanders who led them the right way, and in November 1521, seven months after Magellan's death, the two little ships reached the island of Tidore.

THE GOAL IS ACHIEVED

More than two years had passed since the ships sailed from Spain. Now they were at the group of islands collectively known as the Spice Islands.

The chief of Tidore proved very friendly toward the expedition. He knew a good deal about Europe because he had traded with the Portuguese for several years. The king preferred the Spaniards, he said, to the Portuguese. Trade began immediately.

Tidore is one of the five Spice Islands. The remaining crewmen on the expedition traveled to the Spice Islands after Magellan was killed. The journey took many months.

Cloves take several years to mature. Then they bear spice for the next 20 years. The islanders of Tidore brought load after load of ginger, spice, cinnamon, and nutmeg to the European ships. This was what the intrepid crew members had come around the Earth to obtain.

Around the same time, a Portuguese man presented himself. He had lived on the nearby island of Ternate for several years, and he knew what had happened to Magellan's old friend Francisco Serrao. This man had reached the Spice Islands 10 years earlier and had set himself up as the grand vizier (chief counselor) to the king of Ternate. So successful was Serrao that he made permanent enemies of the leaders of the other Spice Islands. Earlier in 1521, around the same time that Magellan was killed on the beach at Mactan, Serrao was poisoned by the king of Tidore, who was now the host of the Spanish ships.

Nothing could be done about this. The expedition leaders needed to retain the friendship of the king of Tidore.

In mid-December, the two ships were crammed with all the spices they could fit. The two captains announced that they would sail for home. All of the people of Tidore turned out to send them off, but at the last moment it was discovered that the larger of the two ships, the *Trinidad,* was leaking badly.

Here was where the crew members missed Magellan. He was so careful, even fretful, about the condition of his ships that this would not have happened had Magellan been alive.

HEADING HOME

After some days of talks, the crew members decided to split into two groups. The little *Victoria*, captained by Juan Sebastian Elcano, would sail for Spain. The larger *Trinidad,* captained by Juan de Carvalho, would stay in the Spice Islands till it was repaired. Then it too would sail for home.

Antonio Pigafetta decided to sail aboard the *Victoria.* The ship left the Spice Islands on December 21, 1521.

Its captain, Juan Sebastian Elcano, was neither Spanish nor Portuguese, but rather a Basque.

The Basques lived—and still live—in the northern part of Spain and the southwestern part of France. They are an ancient people who have been there a long time, and no one knows where they first came from. In fact, their language is not related to any other European one, making the mystery even deeper.

For centuries, the Basques had been excellent shepherds and fishermen. Juan Sebastian Elcano was an excellent fisherman who became a master sailor. But there was a problem: he had been one of the leaders of the mutiny against Magellan in Port San Julian in 1520.

Beyond doubt, Elcano was an ambitious man. He had not liked Magellan and had tried to overthrow him. But Elcano was also a fine sailor, and the crew members wanted such a man as their new leader. He was no replacement for Magellan, but then, who could have been?

The *Victoria* sailed near the western part of Australia (which the crew members did not see) and headed southeast across the great Indian Ocean.

If Magellan had still been alive, this part of the voyage might have been easier. He knew the Indian Ocean, having been there from 1505 to 1511. He knew something about the tides, the monsoons, and the like. Juan Sebastian Elcano did not know about these things, but he knew enough to pilot his ship through the southern part of this great ocean. There were two reasons he took this route. First, he wanted to avoid Portuguese ships as much

The Cape of Good Hope and Cape Horn

These two capes form two important extensions of land in the Southern Hemisphere. There is not much land between these capes and the continent of Antarctica.

The winds blow very strong in the waters just south of these two capes. There are no landmasses there to break up the winds, which often turn into gales.

Both of the capes are dangerous, but Cape Horn in South America is more so than the Cape of Good Hope. The winds are stronger there, and cut across the decks of sailing ships. For generations, sailors who had made it around the cape called themselves veterans of "Going 'Round the Horn."

There was no choice in those days. In order for people or goods to leave the East Coast of America and reach the West Coast, they had to go 'round the Horn. But at the beginning of the twentieth century, the United States obtained a narrow slip of land in Panama, in Central America. Engineers and laborers worked until 1914, when the new Panama Canal opened for shipping traffic.

as possible, and second, he wanted to sail far enough south so that he could double (get around) the Cape of Good Hope.

Crossing the Indian Ocean was a long, dreary process. Antonio Pigafetta still kept his journal, but he wrote much less about this part of the voyage. This was probably not because there were no sights worth recording, but rather because he and the other crew members were worn out. Not only were they bone-weary from their labors, but they had seen so much death, disease, and hardship along the way that it was difficult to muster enthusiasm for anything new.

As the *Victoria* approached the southern tip of Africa, Captain Elcano became very nervous. He had never doubled the Cape of Good Hope, but he knew from Portuguese records that this was a major achievement in the record of any sailor. There were contrary winds that blew ships about off Africa's southern tip, and for a while it seemed as if the *Victoria* would have to stay in the Indian Ocean forever.

Then came some luck: a change in the winds. After two weeks of helplessly being tossed by

This etching depicts Ferdinand Magellan on his ship *Victoria*. After Magellan's death, Juan Sebastian Elcano captained the *Victoria*, which was the only one of the five original ships to return to Spain.

the waves and winds, the little *Victoria* was able to round the Cape of Good Hope. Having traveled through the Atlantic Ocean, the Strait of Magellan, the Pacific Ocean, the Philippine Islands, and the Indian Ocean, the ship was now back in the Atlantic.

But there were still 5,000 miles to go!

The last part of the voyage was in some ways the hardest. Crew members were exhausted. Captain Elcano had a hard time keeping them under his control. Everyone ached for the voyage to end. But there was still another trial awaiting them.

Off the coast of West Africa, Captain Elcano and the *Victoria* put in to a port to get fresh food and water. A Portuguese captain in the same port learned about their presence and guessed they might belong to the expedition of Ferdinand Magellan. Nearly 20 men were captured while ashore, and they spent years as Portuguese prisoners. Captain Elcano and the others got back on the ship and sailed away.

On September 6, 1522, the little *Victoria* crossed the bar at San Luca and entered the tiny port at the mouth of the Guadalquivir River. The voyage had taken just a little more than three years.

Eighteen Europeans and six Malay Islanders arrived in Spain. The names of the Europeans are enshrined in a monument today:

Juan Sebastian Elcano; Francisco Alba; Michael de Rodas; Juan de Acurio; Martin de Judicibus; Hernando Bustamente; Hans of Aachen; Diego

Carmona; Nicholas the Greek; Miguel Sánchez; Francisco Rodrigues; Juan Rodrigues de Huelva; Antonio Hernandez Colmenero; Juan de Arratia; Vasco Gomes Gallego; Juan de Zubileta; Juan de Santandrés; and, of course, Antonio Pigafetta.[6]

They had arrived!

A REFLECTION

History was not kind to Magellan. For a long time, his mistakes were remembered while his accomplishments were forgotten.

Captain Elcano received a fair amount of praise for bringing the *Victoria* all the way home. He deserved this praise, including a coat of arms with the title, "Thou was the first to encircle Me." But Elcano would never have made it if it were not for Magellan.

Antonio Pigafetta won a great amount of fame for the publication of his journal. History has been kind to Pigafetta. But he, who loved Magellan, would have been the first to point to the captain-general as the reason for the expedition's success.

Life was not kind to the sailors aboard the *Trinidad*. Captain Carvalho took them on a fruitless journey around the Pacific Ocean that ended only when they were captured by Portuguese sailors and thrown into jail. Many of the sailors from the *Trinidad* never made it home.

What of Juan de Cartagena and the priest, who were marooned by Magellan off the coast of South America? They were never heard from again.

What of Magellan's wife? She died of natural causes a few months before the *Victoria* returned to Spain.

When we look at the human tragedy involved, we have to ask: Was it all worth it?

For most of the average sailors, the answer is no. Many of them died, far too high a price for what was achieved.

For the nation of Spain, the answer is again no. Even though Magellan had pioneered a new way to the Spice Islands, King Charles sold whatever right he had to those islands in a treaty with Portugal in 1529.

For Magellan, the answer has to be yes. He devoted his life, his fortunes, and his honor to this mission. Even though he stumbled at the end and died in the Philippines, he achieved his great goal.

For the world, the answer has to be yes. Magellan made it two-thirds of the way, and Elcano finished the job of circumnavigation. The world became a more "known" place after the voyage of 1519–1522.

For human history, the answer is yes. Magellan and his men, despite obstacles, hardships, cruelties, and mistakes, persevered and gave us greater knowledge of the strengths and weaknesses of humankind.

Test Your Knowledge

1 What became of Captain Serrano after Enrique's betrayal?
 a. He was left marooned on the Philippines.
 b. He was killed by the Filipinos.
 c. He was released by the Filipinos after his crew paid a large ransom.
 d. None of the above.

2 Why did the ship, the *Concepcion,* have to be burned?
 a. It was captured by enemy tribesmen.
 b. It was infested with rats.
 c. It was irreparably rotted below the waterline.
 d. None of the above.

3 What spice did Magellan's ships take aboard at Tidore?
 a. Cloves
 b. Ginger
 c. Nutmeg
 d. All of the above

4 Who are the Basques?
 a. An island people of the South Pacific
 b. A people of northern Spain and southern France
 c. Smugglers from Portugal
 d. None of the above

5 The only one of Magellan's ships to return from the Spice Islands to Spain was

a. the *Victoria*.

b. the *Serrano*.

c. the *Concepcion*.

d. the *Trinidad*.

ANSWERS: 1. b; 2. c; 3. d; 4. b; 5. a

1480? Magellan is born in northwest Portugal.

1488 Bartholomew Diaz rounds the Cape of Good Hope.

1492 Spain defeats the Moors; Christopher Columbus sails west and reaches the Bahamas.

1492? Magellan and his brother leave home and go to Lisbon to act as pages.

1493 Pope Alexander VI divides the world into two spheres, one for Spain and one for Portugal.

1498 Vasco da Gama reaches India.

1505 Magellan and his brother sail from Portugal to India.

1480 (?) Magellan is born in northwest Portugal

1492 (?) Magellan and his brother leave home and go to Lisbon to act as pages

1518 King Charles of Spain commissions Magellan to find the Spice Islands

1480

1505 Magellan and his brother sail from Portugal to India; Magellan remains in service in the Indian Ocean till 1511

1516 King Manuel of Portugal turns down Magellan's request to sail to the Spice Islands

1505–1511 Magellan is in service in the Indian Ocean.

1511 Francisco Serrao reaches the Spice Islands.

1513 Magellan goes on an expedition to West Africa.

1516 King Manuel turns down Magellan's request to sail to the Spice Islands.

1517 Magellan arrives in Spain; King Charles arrives in Spain.

1518 King Charles commissions Magellan to find the Spice Islands.

1519 Magellan sails from Spain.

1519 Magellan sails from Spain

1521 Magellan sails the Pacific Ocean, reaching Guam and then the Philippines; he is killed on Mactan Island

1522

1520 Magellan finds the Strait of Magellan

1522 The *Victoria* reaches Spain

1520   Magellan puts down the Easter Mutiny; Magellan finds the Strait; the *San Antonio* mutinies and sails back to Spain.

1521   Magellan sails the Pacific Ocean; Magellan reaches Guam, then the Philippines; Magellan is killed on Mactan Island; the expedition reaches the Spice Islands; the expedition splits, with the *Victoria* and the *Trinidad* sailing separately.

1522   Portuguese ships capture the *Trinidad*; the *Victoria* reaches Spain; Juan Sebastian Elcano is given a special coat of arms with a globe.

1523   Antonio Pigafetta's journal is published.

1529   King Charles sells his interest in the Spice Islands to Portugal.

Chapter 4
The King of Spain

1. Laurence Bergreen. *Over the Edge of the World: Magellan's Terrifying Circumnavigation of the Globe*, New York: William Morrow & Company, 2003, p. 65.

Chapter 5
Magellan in the Atlantic

2. Ibid., p. 94.

Chapter 8
Magellan in the Pacific Ocean

3. Charles E. Nowell, editor, *Magellan's Voyage Around the World: Three Contemporary Accounts*. Evanston, IL: Northwestern University Press, 1962, p. 122

4. Ibid., p. 123.

Chapter 9
Tragedy in the Philippines

5. Laurence Bergreen. *Over the Edge of the World: Magellan's Terrifying Circumnavigation of the Globe*, pp. 281–282.

Chapter 10
Magellan and History

6. Ibid., p. 393.

Bergreen, Laurence. *Over the Edge of the World: Magellan's Terrifying Circumnavigation of the Globe.* New York: William Morrow & Company, 2003.

Joyner, Tim. *Magellan.* Camden, ME: International Marine, 1992.

Nowell, Charles E., editor. *Magellan's Voyage Around the World: Three Contemporary Accounts.* Evanston, IL: Northwestern University Press, 1962.

Smiler Levinson, Nancy. *Magellan and the First Voyage Around the World.* New York: Clarion Books, 2001.

Books

Gallagher, Jim. *Ferdinand Magellan and the First Voyage Around the World.* Philadelphia: Chelsea House Publishers, 2000.

MacDonald, Fiona. *Magellan: A Voyage Around the World.* New York: Franklin Watts, 1998.

Molzahn, Arlene Bourgeois. *Ferdinand Magellan: First Explorer Around the World.* Berkeley Heights, NJ: Enslow, 2003.

Websites

Ferdinand Magellan
http://www.cdli.ca/CITE/exmagellan.htm

Ferdinand Magellan and the First Circumnavigation of the World
http://www.mariner.org/educationalad/ageofex/magellan.php#

Ferdinand Magellan
http://www.ferdinandmagellan.com

Magellan's Voyage Around the World
http://www.socialstudiesforkids.com/articles/worldhistory/magellan1.htm

page:

4: © Réunion des Musées
Nationaux/Art Resource, NY
10: © Bettmann/CORBIS
18: © Foto Marburg/
Art Resource, NY
27: © Sergio Pitamitz/CORBIS
30: © Lindsay Hebberd/
CORBIS
39: © Scala/Art Resource, NY
47: © Gianni Dagli Orti/
CORBIS
55: © MAPS.com/CORBIS
58: © Richard T. Nowitz/
CORBIS

67: © Christophe Loviny/
CORBIS
69: © Giraudon/Art Resource, NY
79: © Wolfgang Kaehler/
CORBIS
85: © Giraudon/Art Resource, NY
91: © Giraudon/Art Resource, NY
97: © Michael S. Yamashita/
CORBIS
105: © Dave G. Houser/CORBIS
109: © Nik Wheeler/CORBIS
117: © Jack Fields/CORBIS
123: © Erich Lessing/
Art Resource, NY

Cover: © Stefano Bianchetti/CORBIS

Samuel Willard Crompton has long had an interest in the sea. He raced small Beetle cat boats in his youth and now sails off the coast of Maine when he has the chance. Crompton teaches American history and Western civilization at Holyoke Community College in his native western Massachusetts. He is the author or editor of more than 30 books, on subjects ranging from lighthouses to wars to spiritual leaders of the world.

William H. Goetzmann is the Jack S. Blanton, Sr., Chair in History and American Studies at the University of Texas, Austin. Dr. Goetzmann was awarded the Joseph Pulitzer and Francis Parkman Prizes for American History, 1967, for *Exploration and Empire: The Explorer and the Scientist in the Winning of the American West.* In 1999, he was elected a member of the American Philosophical Society, founded by Benjamin Franklin in 1743, to honor achievement in the sciences and humanities.